THE ULTIMATE GUIDE

ROBOT WARS™

WARS™ EXTREME™

KAY BARNHAM

PENGUIN BOOKS

mentorn
a television corporation company

THANKS TO ALL THE ROBOTEERS FOR THEIR CONTRIBUTIONS.
A SPECIAL TRIBUTE TO THE LATE DAVID GRIBBLE, DRIVER OF PUSSYCAT.

PENGUIN BOOKS

Published by the Penguin Group
Penguin Books Ltd, 80 Strand, London WC2R 0RL, England
Penguin Putnam Inc., 375 Hudson Street, New York, New York 10014, USA
Penguin Books Australia Ltd, 250 Camberwell Road, Camberwell, Victoria 3124,
Australia
Penguin Books Canada Ltd, 10 Alcorn Avenue, Toronto, Ontario, Canada M4V 3B2
Penguin Books India (P) Ltd, 11 Community Centre, Panchsheel Park, New Delhi –
110 017, India
Penguin Books (NZ) Ltd, Cnr Rosedale and Airborne Roads, Albany, Auckland, New
Zealand
Penguin Books (South Africa) (Pty) Ltd, 24 Sturdee Avenue, Rosebank 2196, South
Africa

Penguin Books Ltd, Registered Offices: 80 Strand, London WC2R 0RL, England

WWW.PENGUIN.COM

First published 2002
3 5 7 9 10 8 6 4 2

CONTENTS

INTRODUCTION

So, you've witnessed the raw power of Robot Wars. You've enjoyed all the damage and the destruction as robots battle each other to the death. But do you really know all there is to know about this mechanical mother of all wars?

The Ultimate Guide is crammed with precise specs and record-breaking stats from the top forty robots to enter the Robot Wars arena. This is not just a list of the highest-scoring robots, but a guide to forty of the most imaginative, the most innovative and simply the most memorable robots – ever! Find out just what your favourite robots are made of – including notes on engine size, clearance, top speed and details of weapons, as well as how they've performed in all the previous wars up until now. It's all here!

But the incredible carnage and destruction in the arena is only the tip of the Robot Wars' iceberg. What goes on behind the scenes? How easy is it to build a battle-worthy robot? How does it feel when your robot is smashed, bashed and totally trashed? Obviously, it's the pits . . .

And what about the mighty House Robots? Shown here for the FIRST TIME EVER are the two new House Robots who will make their debut in the Sixth Wars... Also, their creator, the Chief House Roboteer, has

REVEALED HIS FAVOURITE MOMENTS FROM ROBOT WARS...IS SIR KILLALOT REALLY INVINCIBLE? WHICH WAS SGT BASH'S MOST EXPLOSIVE INFERNO? WHAT HAPPENS WHEN THE ROBOTS FIGHT BACK...?

THE WARS HAVE BEEN LONG AND HARD-FOUGHT. YEAR AFTER YEAR, ROBOTS HAVE ENTERED THE ARENA BUZZING WITH ADRENALIN AND THE WILL TO SUCCEED. SOME HAVE TRIUMPHED. SOME HAVE GONE HOME IN A CARRIER BAG. BUT THEY'RE ALL LISTED HERE IN THIS ESSENTIAL GUIDE TO EVERY ROBOT WARS BATTLE THERE'S EVER BEEN.

FINALLY — FORGET ABOUT THE REST — TAKE A CLOSER LOOK AT THE BEST BATTLES EVER TO BE SHOWN ON TELEVISION, FROM THE MOST VIOLENT, THE QUICKEST AND THE DIRTIEST, TO THE MOST MEMORABLE AND FUNNIEST BATTLES, PLUS THE LONGEST-RUNNING GRUDGE AND THE MOST OUTRAGEOUS REBELLION.

THERE'S NEVER BEEN SO MUCH DATA CRAMMED INTO ONE ROBOT WARS GUIDE! PREPARE TO BE FASCINATED AND RIVETED BY THE MURDEROUS MONSTERS OF MAYHEM...

ARE YOU READY?

STEP UP TO THE ARENA!

THE TEN ROBOT WARS COMMANDMENTS

ROBOTS ARE DANGEROUS, POWERFUL CREATURES, CAPABLE OF MASS DESTRUCTION. AS A RESULT, STRICT GUIDELINES MUST BE OBEYED FOR EACH ROBOT WARS BATTLE. FAILURE TO COMPLY WITH THE RULES LEADS TO INSTANT ELIMINATION. THEY HAVE BEEN WARNED ...

1 A ROBOT MUST BE UNDER CONTROL AT ALL TIMES.

2 A ROBOT MUST NOT BE FITTED WITH A PROJECTILE WEAPON.

3 A ROBOT MUST WEIGH NO MORE THAN 100KG.

4 A ROBOT MUST ACTIVELY ENGAGE IN COMBAT FOR THE DURATION OF EACH FIVE-MINUTE ROUND.

5 A ROBOT MUST NOT PIN THEIR OPPONENT TO THE FLOOR OF THE ARENA OR RESTRAIN THEM FOR MORE THAN ONE MINUTE WHEN ATTACKING WITH A WEAPON.

6 IF TWO OR MORE ROBOTS ARE LOCKED IN A DEADLY EMBRACE, REF BOT WILL SEPARATE THE COMPETITORS AND THE BATTLE WILL CONTINUE.

7 A HOUSE ROBOT MAY ATTACK A ROBOT IF IT ENTERS A CPZ (CORNER PATROL ZONE), BUT THE ATTACK MUST ONLY LAST FIFTEEN SECONDS.

8 IF A ROBOT IS IMMOBILIZED FOR MORE THAN THIRTY SECONDS, THEY ARE ELIMINATED. THE HOUSE ROBOTS ARE THEN FREE TO PERFORM A MERCY KILLING.

9 IF NO ROBOT IS IMMOBILIZED AFTER FIVE MINUTES, THE JUDGES WILL CHOOSE A WINNER AFTER AWARDING EACH ROBOT POINTS FOR STYLE, CONTROL, DAMAGE AND AGGRESSION.

10 IN THE CASE OF A DRAW, THE AUDIENCE'S APPLAUSE DECIDES THE WINNER.

ROBOT WARS TERMINOLOGY

ARENA – ENCLOSED AREA IN WHICH COMBAT TAKES PLACE, ALTERNATIVELY KNOWN AS THE 'COMBAT ARENA' OR THE 'BATTLE ZONE'

CPZ – CORNER PATROL ZONE, WHERE THE HOUSE ROBOTS ARE OFFICIALLY PERMITTED TO JOIN THE FIGHT

DRIVERS – SPECIFIC TERM FOR THOSE INDIVIDUALS WHO CONTROL ROBOTS

EXCESSIVE EVASION – TERM USED TO DESCRIBE THE COWARDLY BEHAVIOUR OF A ROBOT THAT WON'T FIGHT FOR FEAR OF GETTING DESTROYED!

FACE-OFF – A TWO-ROBOT BATTLE

GRUDGE MATCH – A BATTLE FEATURING TWO OR MORE ROBOTS TO SETTLE A DISAGREEMENT OR GRUDGE

HOUSE ROBOTS – THE SHOW'S OWN SUPER ROBOTS, NAMED DEAD METAL, MATILDA, REF BOT, SGT BASH, SHUNT AND SIR KILLALOT

MELEE – A BATTLE FEATURING THREE OR MORE ROBOTS

PITS – BACKSTAGE WORKSHOPS AND STAGING AREA FOR ALL ROBOT WARS EVENTS AND TELEVISION RECORDINGS

PITS MARSHALS – OFFICIALS WHO POLICE THE PITS AREA AND ENSURE HEALTH AND SAFETY POLICIES ARE IMPLEMENTED FULLY

ROBOTEERS – INDIVIDUALS WHO CREATE AND OPERATE ROBOTS

TEST AREA – SEPARATE AREA FOR THE TESTING OF ROBOTS BEFORE COMPETITION OR COMBAT

TRANSMITTER CONTROL – AREA SET ASIDE FOR THE CONTROL AND POLICING OF TRANSMITTERS DURING THE EVENT

WEIGH-IN AREA – WHERE ROBOTS ARE WEIGHED, MEASURED AND PROCESSED

THE DADDY OF T

CHRIS REYNOLDS HAS ONE OF THE MOST POWERFUL,
DESTRUCTIVE AND ENVIABLE JOBS IN ROBOT HISTORY
– HE'S CONTROLLER OF THE HOUSE ROBOTS IN
ROBOT WARS. RESPONSIBLE FOR DESIGNING AND
SUPERVISING THE CONSTRUCTION OF SGT BASH,
MATILDA, SHUNT, DEAD METAL, REF BOT AND SIR
KILLALOT, IT'S UP TO CHRIS TO MAKE SURE THAT
THE HOUSE ROBOTS ARE READY TO RIP THE ROBOT
COMPETITORS TO SHREDS IF THEY DARE TO ENTER
THE CPZ, OR HAVE THE NERVE TO BREAK DOWN.

DID YOU KNOW?

'SGT BASH WAS ORIGINALLY SILVER. ON THE MORNING OF THE
FILMING OF THE FIRST WARS, I DECIDED THAT HE
DIDN'T LOOK WARLIKE ENOUGH. A COUPLE OF CANS OF SPRAY-
PAINT AND SOME MILITARY STRIPES LATER, SGT BASH WAS
TRANSFORMED INTO THE TOUGH, GREEN HOUSE ROBOT
LOATHED BY ROBOTS FAR AND WIDE...'

MOST WORRYING MOMENT

'FIVE MINUTES BEFORE THE THIRD WARS BEGAN, NONE OF THE
HOUSE ROBOTS WAS FUNCTIONING. WE'D USED A NEW INTERFACE
ASSEMBLY, WHICH JUST DIDN'T WORK! LUCKILY, WE MANAGED TO
GET HOLD OF SOME OF THE OLD INTERFACES, AND WITH LESS
THAN FIVE MINUTES BEFORE THE FILMING BEGAN, THE HOUSE
ROBOTS ROARED INTO LIFE.'

FAVOURITE MOMENT

'WHEN SIR KILLALOT APPEARED FOR THE VERY FIRST TIME – AT
THE BEGINNING OF THE SECOND WARS – THE AUDIENCE'S
REACTION WAS ABSOLUTELY AMAZING. SINCE THEN, IT'S FAIR
TO SAY THAT SIR KILLALOT HAS LIVED UP TO THE HYPE.'

FAVOURITE ROBOT

BEING THE FIRST OF THE HOUSE ROBOTS THAT HE DESIGNED,
CHRIS'S FAVOURITE IS SGT BASH. BUT HE ADMITS THAT SIR
KILLALOT IS 'THE BEST' – QUITE SIMPLY BECAUSE HE IS THE
MIGHTIEST.

PROUDEST MOMENT

'WE'D HEARD A RUMOUR THAT THERE WAS GOING TO BE A
REBELLION IN ROBOT WARS EXTREME'S FLIPPER FRENZY. I WAS
CONCERNED THAT SGT BASH AND MATILDA WOULDN'T BE ABLE
TO STAND UP TO AN ATTACK FROM FOUR OF THE BIGGEST

FLIPPERS IN THE GAME, ESPECIALLY IF THEY GANGED UP
TOGETHER. SURE ENOUGH, SGT BASH WAS SOON OVER ON
HIS SIDE, BUT MATILDA AMAZED US ALL. SHE SINGLEHANDED-
LY IMMOBILIZED WHEELY BIG CHEESE, CHAOS 2 AND BIGGER
BROTHER. THERMIDOR II DIDN'T WIN – MATILDA DID!'

FAVOURITE BATTLE TACTIC

'THERE'S NOTHING WORSE THAN A ROBOT WHO STAYS OUT OF
OUR WAY. WE LOVE IT WHEN THEY REALLY GO FOR US. IT
GIVES THE HOUSE ROBOTS A CHANCE TO GET INVOLVED IN
REAL METAL-CRUNCHING, CIRCUIT-RIPPING, ROBOT-IMMOBILIZING
CARNAGE!'

WHAT ABOUT THE NEW HOUSE ROBOTS?

'THEY'RE TOTALLY AWESOME. MR PSYCHO IS A MAD GIANT
ROBOT WITH INCREDIBLE STRENGTH – HE'S NO BRAIN AND ALL
HAMMER! THERE'S SUCH A SENSE OF ANTICIPATION WHEN HE
RAISES HIS ARM IN THE AIR ... THEN THE HAMMER COMES
CRASHING DOWN TO DESTROY WHATEVER'S BENEATH! AND
GROWLER THE DOG IS SUPERB. HE USES A SKID STEER
SYSTEM THAT MEANS HE'S FAST AND VERY MANOEUVRABLE –
VERY EFFECTIVE WHEN HE WANTS TO BITE A ROBOT AND THEN
GET OUT OF THERE!

MATILDA

WEIGHT	LENGTH
116KG	1.4M

WIDTH	HEIGHT
0.66M	0.66M

SPEED	POWER
8MPH	12 VOLT MOTOR, RECHARGEABLE BATTERY UNIT, TUSKS POWERED BY POWERFUL PNEUMATIC SYSTEM

WEAPONS

HYDRAULIC TUSKS FOR LIFTING, SHUNTING OR PIERCING, AND A TAIL-MOUNTED CHAINSAW TO SLICE AND DICE. CHAINSAW IS INTERCHANGE-ABLE WITH A STATE-OF-THE-ART FLYWHEEL WEAPON THAT WEIGHS OVER 25KG.

BACKSTAGE GOSSIP:
MATILDA HAD HER FINEST MOMENT DURING FLIPPER FRENZY IN ROBOT WARS EXTREME. CHAOS 2, WHEELY BIG CHEESE, BIGGER BROTHER AND THERMIDOR II TOOK PART IN AN OUTRAGEOUS REBELLION AGAINST MATILDA AND SGT BASH. SGT BASH WAS SOON OVER AND OUT, BUT MATILDA WALTZED INTO ACTION . . . WITH ONE WALLOP, SHE IMMOBILIZED WHEELY BIG CHEESE, THEN DID THE SAME TO CHAOS 2 AND FINALLY BIGGER BROTHER. THERMIDOR II WERE LEFT SCUTTLING AROUND THE ARENA, LOOKING FOR SOMEWHERE TO HIDE!

HOUSE ROBOTS

SHUNT

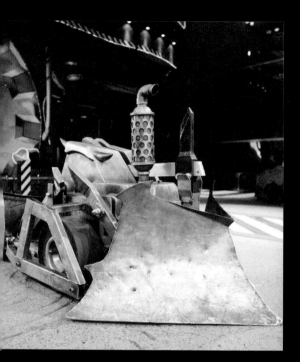

WEIGHT	105KG
LENGTH	1.3M
WIDTH	1.1M
HEIGHT	0.7M
SPEED	10MPH

POWER

SCOOP AND AXE POWERED BY PRESSURIZED CARBON DIOXIDE. CAN DRAG A LOADED LAND ROVER FROM A STANDING START TO A SPEED OF 6MPH.

WEAPONS

DIAMOND-EDGED AXE HITS WITH A FORCE OF 500KG PER CM². BULLDOZING SHOVELS FRONT AND REAR HAVE BEEN REDESIGNED FOR EXTRA STRENGTH.

BACKSTAGE GOSSIP:

ONE OF SHUNT'S BEST MOMENTS TOOK PLACE DURING A FIGHT BETWEEN HYPNO-DISC AND PUSSYCAT IN THE GRAND FINAL OF THE FOURTH WARS. PUSSYCAT HAD PUSHED HYPNO-DISC INTO THE CPZ, WHERE SHUNT SLAMMED HIS AXE INTO THE FAMOUS SPINNING WHEEL – STOPPING IT DEAD IN ITS TRACKS.

DEAD METAL

WEIGHT	112kg
LENGTH	1.6m
WIDTH	1m
HEIGHT	0.7m
SPEED	12mph
POWER	Battery driven, with pneumatically powered pincers

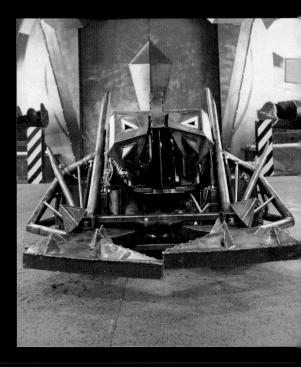

WEAPONS

3000rpm circular saw has been redesigned for added durability. Grasping claws have been rebuilt for greater strength.

Backstage gossip:

Dead Metal really made sparks fly when he once cut into one of Wheely Big Cheese's wheels. The wheels are covered in titanium-tipped spikes and when Dead Metal's huge circular saw came into blistering contact with them, it was as if the arena had turned into a fireworks display area!

HOUSE ROBOTS

SIR KILLALOT

WEIGHT	LENGTH
280KG	1.2M

WIDTH	HEIGHT
1.2M	1.3M

SPEED	POWER
8MPH	COMBUSTION ENGINE FUELLED BY PETROL WITH HYDRAULIC POWER TO WEAPONS. DRIVE MECHANISM REBUILT TO INCREASE POWER TO THE TRACKS.

WEAPONS

POWER LANCE ON ONE ARM AND PIERCING JAWS ON THE OTHER. THREE TIMES AS HEAVY AS MOST COMBATANTS.

BACKSTAGE GOSSIP:

SIR KILLALOT IS INVINCIBLE. OR IS HE? HE HAS FLUNG CONTENDERS FAR AND WIDE, BUT THERE HAVE BEEN ONE OR TWO CHINKS IN HIS ARMOUR... PUSSYCAT, MORTIS AND RAZER HAVE ALL HAD A GO AT SIR KILLALOT, BUT ONE OF THE MOST REMARKABLE ATTACKS WAS BY PITBULL IN THE THIRD WARS. THEY RAMMED INTO THE SIDE OF THE HEAVYWEIGHT HOUSE ROBOT, SUCCEEDING IN SNAPPING ONE OF SIR KILLALOT'S HYDRAULIC HOSES. THAT WAS IT – ALL WEAPONS IMMOBILIZED AND OIL EVERYWHERE. IT WON'T HAPPEN AGAIN THOUGH. SIR KILLALOT IS NOW MORE INVINCIBLE THAN EVER...

SGT BASH

WEIGHT	120KG
LENGTH	1.4M
WIDTH	0.9M
HEIGHT	0.9M
SPEED	5MPH

POWER

POWERED BY FOUR MASSIVE BATTERIES, PNEUMATICALLY DRIVEN WITH PROPANE-FUELLED FLAMETHROWER

WEAPONS

TURRET-MOUNTED FLAMETHROWER UPGRADED TO SUPER-BARBECUE POWER FRONT PINCER REDESIGNED TO BECOME SURGICAL STEEL JAWS FOR ADDED BITE. REAR-MOUNTED CUTTING DISC MEANS HE CAN ATTACK IN ANY DIRECTION.

BACKSTAGE GOSSIP:

DURING ROBOT WARS, SGT BASH HAS ROASTED, TOASTED AND TORCHED DIÓTÓIR VIRTUALLY EVERY TIME THEY'VE MET, BUT HE WAS ALSO RESPONSIBLE FOR A FLAMING SPECTACULAR IN THE FIFTH WARS. GRANNY'S REVENGE – A VERY TALL, VERY FLAMMABLE ROBOT – WAS JUST ASKING FOR IT ... SGT BASH FIRED THE FLAMETHROWER AND TRANSFORMED GRANNY INTO GUY FAWKES. IT WAS BONFIRE NIGHT AT ROBOT WARS!

REF BOT

WEIGHT	120KG
LENGTH	1.4M
WIDTH	0.9M
HEIGHT	1.3M
SPEED	7MPH
POWER	ELECTRIC MOTOR, BATTERY POWERED

WEAPONS

BULLDOZING SHUNTS, FRONT AND REAR, TO SEPARATE ROBOTS THAT BECOME LOCKED IN MORTAL COMBAT. ELECTRONIC COUNTDOWN BOARD MOUNTED ON CHEST AND LIGHT-INDICATOR SYSTEM ON LEFT ARM. PINCER GRIP ON LEFT ARM AND FIRE EXTINGUISHER ON THE RIGHT.

BACKSTAGE GOSSIP:

REF BOT IS A FINE, UPSTANDING MEMBER OF THE HOUSE ROBOTS TEAM. HE'S RESPONSIBLE FOR REFEREEING FIGHTS, BREAKING UP DEADLY EMBRACES, COUNTING OUT IMMOBILIZED ROBOTS, PUTTING OUT FIRES AND (IF NECESSARY) SHOWING YELLOW OR RED CARDS. NO UNDERHAND DEALINGS, NO CARNAGE — NOTHING WILL SLIP PAST THIS UNFLINCHING REFEREE.

BRAND NEW

MR
PSYCHO

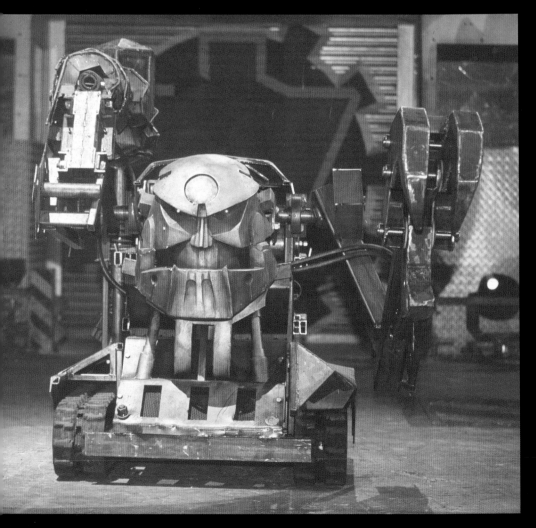

House Robot

WEIGHT	**LENGTH**
600KG	2.1M
WIDTH	**HEIGHT**
1.45M	1.5M
SPEED	**POWER**
8MPH	12 BATTERIES POWER THE TWO 36V ELECTRIC LYNCH MOTORS

WEAPONS

POWERFUL GRABBING HAND ON ONE ARM PRODUCES A FORCE OF 3 TONNES. OTHER ARM IS EQUIPPED WITH A 30KG HAMMER, CAPABLE OF BASHING AT SPEEDS UP TO 60MPH.

BACKSTAGE GOSSIP:

BRAND SPANKING NEW FOR THE SIXTH WARS, MR PSYCHO IS THE HEAVIEST HOUSE ROBOT — EVER. BUT HE'S ALSO A BIT OF A TROUBLEMAKER... HE ALREADY HAS A REPUTATION FOR WRECKING EVERYTHING THAT HE COMES INTO CONTACT WITH — ROBOTS, THE ARENA, EVEN HIMSELF! HE'S A PSYCHOTIC LUMP OF METAL — AND HE'S DETERMINED TO CREATE CARNAGE. BEWARE...

BRAND NEW
GROWLER

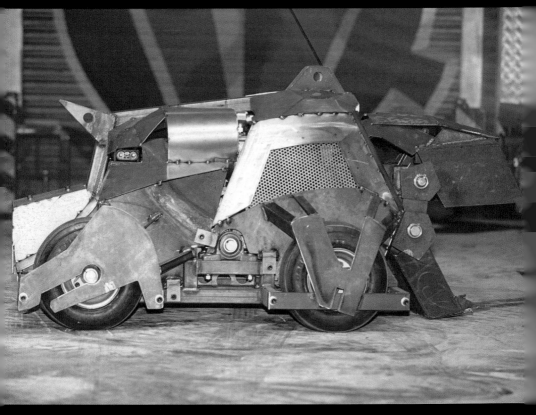

HOUSE ROBOT

WEIGHT	**LENGTH**
420KG	1.5M
WIDTH	**HEIGHT**
1.1M	0.7M
SPEED	**POWER**
20MPH	12 BATTERIES POWER THE TWO 36V ELECTRIC LYNCH MOTORS

WEAPONS

HYDRAULICALLY POWERED JAWS CAPABLE OF CRUSHING WITH A PRESSURE OF 4 TONNES.

BACKSTAGE GOSSIP:

ALSO NEW FOR THE SIXTH WARS, GROWLER IS MR PSYCHO'S SNAPPING, SNARLING SIDEKICK. CAPABLE OF GRABBING A 100KG ROBOT IN HIS JAWS, SHAKING IT AROUND AND THEN DUMPING IT IN THE PIT, THIS IS NO CUDDLY PUPPY. HE'S FAST, HE'S FEROCIOUS — AND HE'S GOT AN AWESOME BITE...

101

FORMER INCARNATIONS: ROBO-DOC

TRACKS ARE MORE FUN WITH 101

WEIGHT	HEIGHT
90KG	0.4M

LENGTH	SPEED
1.03M	10MPH

WIDTH	CLEARANCE
0.94M	2MM

POWER	WEAPONS
12V ELECTRIC MOTORS	VERTICALLY MOUNTED SPINNING FLYWHEEL

TEAM (KETTERING)

MIKE FRANKLIN (CAPTAIN), AMY FRANKLIN AND
STEVE BICKLE

Team Battle History

Second Wars: (As Robo-Doc) ran riot through the heat, before losing to King Buxton in the third task on a judges' decision.

Third Wars: Fought through to the semi-finals, after narrowly defeating King Buxton. 101 won on points. Won round 1 of semi-finals by shunting Scutter's Revenge into House Robots. An epic battle with Hypno-Disc followed in round 2 of the semi-finals, but a judges' decision went against 101.

Fourth Wars: Shunted Major Tom into the arena wall to reach heat final, where judges awarded the match to Dominator II. Winner of the Fourth Wars Tag-Team contest with King B3.

Fifth Wars: When Fluffy ripped off one of their tracks, it was all over for 101 in round 1 of the heats.

Extreme: Competed in UK Tag Team and beat King B Powerworks in a Vengeance battle.

Best moment: The Third Wars when 101 made it to the heady heights of the semi-finals.

Worst moment: After the heavy-duty battling of previous wars, quite a lot of work went into repairing, improving and preparing 101 for the Fifth Wars. The philosophy behind 101's design is that wear and tear will happen. The aim is to make sure that the robot withstands damage long enough to retaliate – and inflict the same punishment on the opponent. So, as you can imagine, the team was devastated to be dispatched from the Fifth Wars in round 1 by a complete novice...

Web site: www.robot101.fsnet.co.uk/default.html

ROBOT PROFILES

3 STEGS TO HEAVEN

FORMER INCARNATIONS: STEG-O-SAW-US, STEG 2

LEAN, MEAN AND GREEN . . .

WEIGHT	HEIGHT
96KG	0.24M

LENGTH	SPEED
1.12M	16MPH

WIDTH	CLEARANCE
0.79M	10MM

POWER	WEAPONS
24V ELECTRIC MOTOR	SPINNING CUTTER

TEAM (SOUTHAMPTON)

PETER ROWE (CAPTAIN), DANNY KING AND RICHARD FRANCIS

22

TEAM BATTLE HISTORY

THIRD WARS: (As Steg-o-Saw-Us) thrashing Napalm in the heat final was only the first step towards the grand final, where Hypno-Disc triumphed after breaking one of Steg's tracks.

FOURTH WARS: (As Steg 2) in a classic semi-final battle, Chaos 2 eventually flipped Steg 2 to win, going on to become the eventual Grand Champions.

FIFTH WARS: Briefly entangled with Eleven in round 1, had a lucky win over the aggressive Tetanus in the next round, but could do nothing against Bigger Brother in the heat final.

EXTREME: Competed in UK All Star.

BEST MOMENT: The Fourth Wars went tremendously well for Steg 2. They were seeded seventh and really lived up to their reputation, brutally knocking out Cronos, Iron Awe and Mortis on the way to the semi-finals.

WORST MOMENT: Being drawn against current Grand Champions, Chaos 2, in the semi-finals of the Fourth Wars . . .

WEB SITE: WWW.GEOCITIES.COM/STEG_TEAM/

AGGROBOT III

FORMER INCARNATIONS: AGGROBOT, AGGROBOT II

JUST DON'T AGGRAVATE THEM, RIGHT?

WEIGHT	HEIGHT
99KG	0.35M

LENGTH	SPEED
1.4M	10MPH

WIDTH	CLEARANCE
0.94M	25MM

POWER	WEAPONS
3 x 12V ELECTRIC MOTORS	SHEARS AND WEDGE-SHAPED LIFTER

TEAM (DORKING)

PETER LEACH (CAPTAIN), BOB LEACH AND JOHN LEACH

TEAM BATTLE HISTORY

THIRD WARS: (AS AGGROBOT) DAMAGE INFLICTED BY RAZER IN THEIR HEAT RESULTED IN AGGROBOT'S BREAKDOWN IN THE HEAT FINAL. TO ADD INSULT TO INJURY, THEY WERE FINALLY SHUNTED ON TO THE FLAME PIT, WHERE THEY FRIED...

FOURTH WARS: (AS AGGROBOT II) SPENT ROUND 2 OF HEAT BEING SHUNTED AND RAMMED INTO OBLIVION BY S.M.I.D.S.Y.

EXTREME: (AS AGGROBOT III) COMPETED IN UK MAYHEM. STARTED WELL, TURNING SPLINTER ON TO THEIR SIDE, BUT AGGROBOT'S LIFTER JAMMED FULLY OPEN TO IMMOBILIZE THEM. A SQUEEZE FROM SIR KILLALOT RESTARTED AGGROBOT, BUT THEY LOST ON A JUDGES' DECISION.

BACKSTAGE GOSSIP: IT'S AGGROBOT'S AMBITION TO PAY BACK SIR KILLALOT FOR THE DAMAGE HE'S INFLICTED ON THEM IN THE PAST, TO GIVE MATILDA A GOOD DRESSING DOWN AND TO BEAT RAZER FAIR AND SQUARE.

BEST MOMENT: BEATING RAZER IN THE SECOND ROUND OF THE THIRD WAR AFTER BEING LABELLED THE UNDERDOGS. NO ONE BELIEVED THEY COULD DO IT – EXCEPT THE TEAM. RAZER JUST COULDN'T GET A GRIP ON AGGROBOT AND KEPT SLIDING OFF. FINALLY, AGGROBOT MANAGED TO FIRE THE SPIKE INTO RAZER'S WORKINGS – AND WON!

WORST MOMENT: BREAKING DOWN AND LOSING THE NEXT BATTLE BECAUSE THERE WAS NO TIME TO FIX AGGROBOT II PROPERLY, DESPITE WORKING ROUND THE CLOCK...

ATOMIC II

FORMER INCARNATIONS: ATOMIC

A FLIPPING GREAT ROBOT!

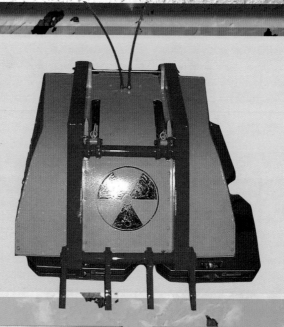

WEIGHT 100KG		**HEIGHT** 0.4M
LENGTH 0.9M		**SPEED** 12MPH
WIDTH 0.75M		**CLEARANCE** 5MM
POWER 24V ELECTRIC MOTORS		**WEAPONS** LETHAL SPIKE AND ADJUSTABLE FLIPPER

TEAM (ARLEY, WORCESTER)

STEPHEN BEBB (CAPTAIN), PAUL FRANCIS AND
DAVID BEBB

TEAM BATTLE HISTORY

FOURTH WARS: (As ATOMIC) BEAT VETERAN OF TWO PREVIOUS WARS, KING B3, TO MEET CHAOS 2 IN HEAT FINAL. THE EVENTUAL GRAND CHAMPIONS FLIPPED ATOMIC AROUND THE ARENA, BEFORE THEY WERE WELL AND TRULY FINISHED OFF BY SIR KILLALOT.

FIFTH WARS: EFFORTLESSLY FLIPPED KAN OPENER IN FIRST ROUND, BUT HAD A VERY CLOSE ENCOUNTER WITH HYPNO-DISC'S DEADLY SPINNING DISC IN ROUND 2 OF HEAT...

EXTREME: WON THROUGH TO ANNIHILATOR ROUND OF UK MAYHEM, BUT WERE FORCED TO RETIRE.

BEST MOMENT: FIRST EVER BATTLE WITH ATOMIC AGAINST REACTOR IN THE FOURTH WARS QUALIFIER. THE TEAM HAD NO IDEA HOW THE ROBOT WOULD PERFORM IN BATTLE, BUT MANAGED TO FLIP REACTOR ALL AROUND THE ARENA AND, IN THE DYING SECONDS OF THE FIGHT, FLIPPED THEM RIGHT OUT!

WORST MOMENT: AGAINST CHAOS 2 IN THEIR FOURTH WARS HEAT FINAL. ATOMIC WERE FLIPPED ABOUT SIX TIMES BY CHAOS 2 IN AN ATTEMPT TO GET THEM OUT OF THE ARENA, AND THEN SIR KILLALOT PICKED THEM UP AND FINALLY ATTACKED THEM WITH THEIR HYDRAULIC CLAW. NOT ONLY WERE ATOMIC DEFEATED, THEY SUFFERED SEVERE BATTLE DAMAGE...

BEHEMOTH

A MONSTROUS CREATURE!

WEIGHT	HEIGHT
98KG	0.4M

LENGTH	SPEED
1.15M	7MPH

WIDTH	CLEARANCE
0.62M	15MM

POWER	WEAPONS
24V ELECTRIC MOTORS	PNEUMATIC SCOOP

TEAM (HEMEL HEMPSTEAD)

ANTHONY PRITCHARD (CAPTAIN), MICHAEL PRITCHARD AND KANE ASTON

Team Battle History

Second Wars: Smashed by Killertron in the semi-finals.

Third Wars: Fought Pit Bull in heat final, but were soon at the mercy of the House Robots. Lost on points.

Fourth Wars: Controversial judges' decision awarded round 3 of heat to X-Terminator instead of Behemoth.

Fifth Wars: Won a tough battle against Supernova to reach round 2 of heat, where Crushtacean tossed them, rammed them and then pushed them into the pit.

Extreme: Competed in UK Mayhem and Wild Card, beat Steel Avenger and Stinger in Challenge Belt and reached All Stars quarter-final.

Best moment: Nearly winning the Robot Wars First World Championship. Well, runners-up isn't bad, is it?!

Worst moment: Having added an axe, Behemoth thought they were in with a real chance in the Fifth Wars. They were looking good, so tried to flip Crushtacean over, but landed on top of them, so Crushtacean were able to lever Behemoth over instead. Not one of Behemoth's greatest moments...

Web site: www.teambehemoth.co.uk

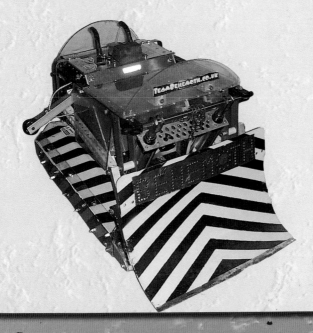

BIGGER BROTHER

FORMER INCARNATIONS: BIG BROTHER

NO GUTS, NO GLORY!

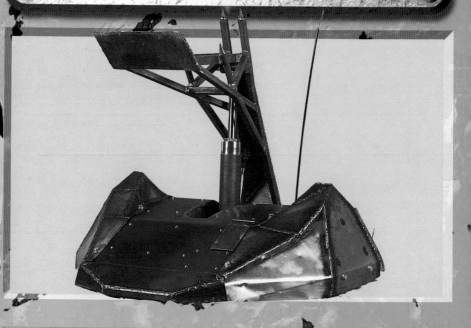

WEIGHT	HEIGHT
99KG	0.91M

LENGTH	SPEED
0.8M	12MPH

WIDTH	CLEARANCE
0.8M	0 MM

POWER	WEAPONS
2 x 750W ELECTRIC MOTORS	SPIKED CO_2- POWERED FLIPPER

TEAM (BRIGHTON)

JOE WATTS (CAPTAIN), IAN WATTS AND ELLIE WATTS

TEAM BATTLE HISTORY

THIRD WARS: (AS BIG BROTHER) RAMMED AND FLIPPED THEIR WAY TO THE SEMI-FINALS, WHERE MACE II FLIPPED THEM STRAIGHT INTO SGT BASH...

FOURTH WARS: A CO_2 LEAK LED TO WEAPON FAILURE IN ROUND 2 OF HEAT, WHEN BULLDOG BREED II FLIPPED THEM TO WIN.

FIFTH WARS: BIGGER BROTHER HAD AN EASY ROUTE TO THE SEMI-FINALS, SENDING BOTH TIP-TOP AND SPLINTER OUT OF THE ARENA, BEFORE OUT-CLASSING 3 STEGS TO HEAVEN IN THE HEAT FINAL. AS AN ENCORE, THEY FLIPPED SHUNT! IN THE SEMI-FINALS, BIGGER BROTHER WERE AGGRESSIVE FROM THE START, EASILY FLIPPING S3. THEY MET CHAOS 2 IN THE NEXT ROUND, BUT PLAYED A TACTICAL FIGHT, WAITING UNTIL THEIR OPPONENTS RAN OUT OF GAS BEFORE FLIPPING TO WIN! THROUGH TO THE GRAND FINAL, THEY WERE BATTERED AND BASHED BY HYPNO-DISC, BUT REFUSED TO GIVE UP AND EVENTUALLY PUSHED THEM DOWN THE PIT. BIGGER BROTHER HAD ENORMOUS STAYING POWER IN THE GRAND FINAL, BUT JUST COULDN'T DO AS MUCH DAMAGE AS RAZER...

EXTREME: COMPETED IN FLIPPER FRENZY, UK TAG TEAM AND WON THEIR VENGEANCE BATTLE.

WORST MOMENT: THIS WAS DURING THE FOURTH WARS, WHEN THE GAS UNION LET THEM DOWN IN THE SECOND ROUND AND THEY LOST TO BULLDOG BREED II.

BEST MOMENT: WHAT BIGGER BROTHER CONSIDER TO BE THE MOST AWESOME BATTLE IN THE HISTORY OF ROBOT WARS IS THEIR FIGHT AGAINST HYPNO-DISC. THEY TOOK A TREMENDOUS AMOUNT OF PUNISHMENT, BUT STILL CLAIMED A VICTORY. THEY HAD TO FIGHT AGAIN IN A FEW HOURS AND THERE WAS AN ENORMOUS AMOUNT OF DAMAGE TO FIX, BUT EVERYONE PITCHED IN. AND FOUR HOURS LATER BIGGER BROTHER WERE READY TO ENTER THE ARENA ONCE MORE...

WEB SITE: WWW.TEAMBIGBRO.CO.UK

BULLDOG BREED III

FORMER INCARNATIONS: BULLDOG BREED, BULLDOG BREED II

RAM AND FLIP

WEIGHT	HEIGHT
98KG	0.3M

LENGTH	SPEED
1.95M	15MPH

WIDTH	CLEARANCE
0.7M	8MM

POWER	WEAPONS
24V ELECTRIC MOTOR	FLIPPER AND REAR TWIN-TAILED HARDENED SPIKES

TEAM (CANNOCK)

TONY SOMERFIELD (CAPTAIN), SEAN BOND AND ROBERT SOMERFIELD

Team Battle History

Third Wars: (As Bulldog Breed) defeated by Robopig (and Shunt!) in round 1 of heat.

Fourth Wars: (As Bulldog Breed II) reached heat final, but Stinger inflicted major damage to armour and flipping arm.

Fifth Wars: Flipped and rammed Juggernot II, then roasted Lambsy, winning on points. Put up a good fight against Hypno-Disc, until the deadly spinning disc ripped out Bulldog's safety switch, causing instant immobilization.

Extreme: Competed in UK Mayhem, reaching Annihilator round, but had to pull out.

Backstage Gossip: Bulldog Breed III's most memorable Robot Wars moment didn't happen in the arena – it was in the back of their car! They were on the way to driving practice when the remote control fell off the rear seat... and because the robot's safety switch hadn't been adjusted, it sent Bulldog Breed into a terrifying high-speed spin. Bulldog Breed survived the incident but the back of the car suffered some serious battle damage!

Web site: www.bulldog-breed.co.uk

CHAOS 2

FORMER INCARNATIONS: ROBOT THE BRUCE, CHAOS

HIT 'EM AND FLIP 'EM

WEIGHT	HEIGHT
85KG	0.4M

LENGTH	SPEED
0.9M	20MPH

WIDTH	CLEARANCE
0.74M	1MM

POWER	WEAPONS
24V ELECTRIC MOTOR	VERTICALLY MOUNTED SPINNING FLYWHEEL

TEAM (IPSWICH)

GEORGE FRANCIS (CAPTAIN), IAN SWANN AND RICHARD SWANN

Team Battle History

First Wars: (As Robot the Bruce) powered their way to the grand final, where they fell victim to Road Block.

Second Wars: (As Chaos) defeated by Mace in heat final, after Shunt and Matilda had their wicked way.

Third Wars: Grand champions! On the road to victory, Chaos 2 flipped Mace II, Firestorm and Hypno-Disc, before flipping Matilda and Shunt — just because they could! Chaos 2 became the first robot to toss another out of the arena.

Fourth Wars: Stinger inflicted damage on to their rear armour in the grand final, but Chaos 2 won on points. Then, despite more damage from Pussycat, they won the judges' decision and were Grand Champions for a record-breaking second time!

Fifth Wars: Flipped Storm Force into the pit in round 1 before really going for it with Steel Avenger, whose 20mm clearance allowed Chaos 2 to flip them right out of the arena. Came pretty close to losing to S.M.I.D.S.Y. in the heat final, but won on a rematch. The first round was nail-biting, with Chaos 2 twice scrambling out of the pit of doom to beat Wild Thing on a judges' decision. Their luck ran out in the next round, when they didn't have enough power to self-right after Bigger Brother flipped them. They were Grand Champions no more.

Extreme: Winners of Netherlands v UK, competed in Flipper Frenzy and Challenge Belt. Beaten in All Stars semi-final by Tornado.

Best moment: Fight against Wild Thing in round 1 of the semi-finals in the Fifth Wars. Chaos 2 were pushed in the pit TWICE, scrambling out each time with frantic remote controlling!

Worst moment: In the heat final of the Fifth Wars, when Chaos 2 wedged S.M.I.D.S.Y. against the side of the arena and then accidentally flipped over them-selves. As hard as they tried, they couldn't self-right and S.M.I.D.S.Y. were gradually wiggling back on to the arena floor. Luckily, time ran out and the judges called for a rematch.

Web site: www.gt-electronics.freeserve.co.uk/index.htm

DIÓTÓIR

FORMER INCARNATIONS: NEMESIS

ROBOT WARS'
FAVOURITE INFERNO . . .

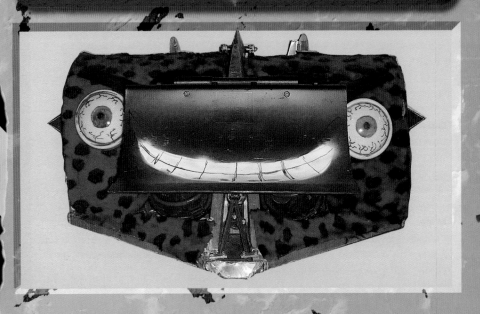

WEIGHT	HEIGHT
92KG	0.39M

LENGTH	SPEED
1.17M	6MPH

WIDTH	CLEARANCE
1.04M	0MM

POWER	WEAPONS
36V ELECTRIC MOTOR	FLIPPER

TEAM (DUBLIN)

PETER REDMOND (CAPTAIN), DR ZULU AND JOE GAVIN

TEAM BATTLE HISTORY

FIRST WARS: (As Nemesis) lost to Road Block on points in third task of heat, after being set upon by all the House Robots. Went up in flames thanks to Sgt Bash.

SECOND WARS: (As Nemesis) torched by Sgt Bash again en route to the third task of the heat. Entered the arena with a kebab attached (ready for roasting!), but Diótóir didn't get cooked and ended up in the pit instead.

THIRD WARS: Lost to Firestorm in heat final, after being set alight by Sgt Bash as usual...

FOURTH WARS: Went up in flames in round 1 of heat.

FIFTH WARS: Flipped and immobilized The Dome within seconds. A tough second-round battle against Tornado ended when Diótóir pushed them into the pit. Met Spawn Again in the heat final, but were tossed on to their back. Diótóir's self-righting mechanism made their eyes pop out, but couldn't turn them over – then Sgt Bash torched the furry Irish robot. Again.

EXTREME: Winners (with Pussycat) of UK Tag Team, competed in UK All Stars, UK Mayhem and Vengeance.

BEST MOMENT: Winning the Sportsmanship Award for the third time!

WORST MOMENT: Being knocked out of the Fourth Wars. They travelled overnight from Dublin to be told that they were the next to fight, only to discover that Diótóir was 6kg overweight. To lose the weight, they lost the armour, but then had problems with the settings on Diótóir's ram. The chain connecting the mechanism snapped. It was repaired but snapped again. And then it was time to go on... With no armour and no weapon they went into battle – and lasted about four seconds.

WEB SITE: WWW.ESATCLEAR.IE/~FEORAS/DIOTOIR/

AWARDS
SPORTSMANSHIP AWARD (FIRST WARS)
SPORTSMANSHIP AWARD (THIRD WARS)
SPORTSMANSHIP AWARD (FOURTH WARS)

DOMINATOR II

FORMER INCARNATIONS: DOMINATOR

WITH AN AXE OF DOOM...

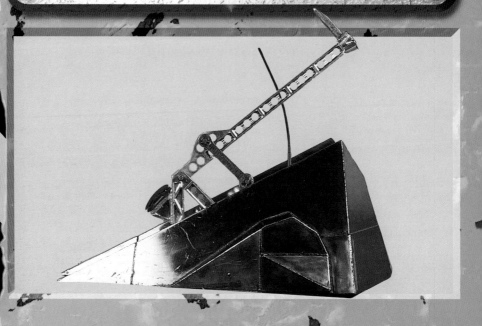

WEIGHT	HEIGHT
100KG	1.14M

LENGTH	SPEED
1.4M	20MPH

WIDTH	CLEARANCE
0.78M	1MM

POWER	WEAPONS
2 x 750W ELECTRIC MOTORS	PNEUMATIC AXE

TEAM (HUNTINGDON)

PETER HALLOWAY (CAPTAIN), ELLIOT SMART AND CHRIS HALL

Team Battle History

Third Wars: (As Dominator) came second to Razer in Pinball Tournament.

Fourth Wars: Dominated Shadow of Napalm and 101 to reach the semi-finals. Seemed as if Firestorm were getting the upper hand, but Dominator II recovered to jam their axe into Firestorm's flipping blade, winning on points. The next battle turned into a real cat fight, with Pussycat biting and scratching their way to victory.

Fifth Wars: Stormed through the heats by jamming Derek into the arena wall, perforating King B Powerwork's armour and spinning around with Corkscrew. Reached the semi-finals by surviving one of Wheely Big Cheese's legendary flips and winning when the Cheese conked out. The next round started with Hypno-Disc ripping off Dominator II's side, then staying out of the way to avoid damage. A very tactical fight, said by the judges to be the most boring fight ever...

Extreme: Competed in UK All Stars and won a Wild Card battle.

Backstage Gossip: Once, while testing Dominator, Elliot drove the robot straight at his own car. The front tyre was no match for Dominator's front tips...

Best moment: In the Fifth Wars, when they were flipped about three metres high in the air by Wheely Big Cheese – and then landed on top of Cheese, taking particular pleasure in penetrating their beloved titanium shell.

Worst moment: When Dominator II 'died' in the final moments of the Fourth Wars Annihilator, after dishing out serious punishment to the other contestants.

Web site: www.team-dominator.co.uk

FIRESTORM 3

FORMER INCARNATIONS: GROUNDHOG, FIRESTORM, FIRESTORM 2

STRONGER, TOUGHER – AND GUARANTEED TO CAUSE A STORM

WEIGHT	HEIGHT
100KG	0.31M

LENGTH	SPEED
1.05M	12MPH

WIDTH	CLEARANCE
0.9M	1MM

POWER	WEAPONS
36V ELECTRIC MOTOR	FLIPPING ARM WITH KINETIC WEAPONRY

TEAM (DURHAM)

GRAHAM BONE (CAPTAIN), ALEX MORDUE AND HAZEL HESLOP

TEAM BATTLE HISTORY

SECOND WARS: (AS GROUNDHOG) KNOCKED OUT IN THIRD TASK OF HEAT, BUT NOT BEFORE TOPPLING SIR KILLALOT!

THIRD WARS: (AS FIRESTORM) REACHED GRAND FINAL (TOASTING DIÓTÓIR AND DEAD METAL ON THE WAY), BUT COULDN'T OUTDO CHAOS 2.

FOURTH WARS: (AS FIRESTORM 2) DEFEATED IN SEMI-FINALS BY DOMINATOR II, IN WHAT WAS SAID TO BE ONE OF THE CLOSEST BATTLES EVER.

FIFTH WARS: HAD A FLIPPING MARVELLOUS TIME IN THE HEATS WITH BEE-CAPITATOR, SIR CHROMALOT (ONE OF THE FASTEST WINS EVER) AND REACTOR II, WHO WERE CATAPULTED RIGHT OUT OF THE ARENA. KNOCKED OUT OF THE SEMI-FINALS BY HYPNO-DISC WHEN THEIR FLIPPER FAILED TO FUNCTION BUT, AFTER FRENZIED REPAIRS, THEY TOOK PART IN THE LOSERS' MELEE TO WIN THROUGH TO THE GRAND FINAL. IT WAS BACK TO THE DRAWING BOARD WHEN RAZER ELIMINATED THEM AFTER ONE OF THE CLOSEST FIGHTS EVER BUT, IN THE PLAY-OFF, FIRESTORM WREAKED THEIR REVENGE IN A FANTASTIC BATTLE AGAINST HYPNO-DISC TO WIN THIRD PLACE!

EXTREME: REACHED THE ALL STARS SEMI-FINALS AND WON THEIR VENGEANCE BATTLE AGAINST DIÓTÓIR.

BEST MOMENT: THE WHOLE OF THE FIFTH WARS WAS FANTASTIC FROM START TO FINISH. THEY STORMED THROUGH THE HEATS AND THE SEMI-FINALS, AND EVENTUALLY CAME THIRD OUT OF THE WHOLE TOURNAMENT.

WORST MOMENT: WHEN THE TEAM LEARNED AN IMPORTANT LESSON ABOUT THE CORRECT ORDER IN WHICH TO TURN FIRESTORM'S TRANSMITTERS AND RECEIVERS ON. IF YOU TURN THE RECEIVER ON FIRST, THERE'S A GOOD CHANCE THE FLIPPER WILL FIRE ALL BY ITSELF. THIS ALMOST COST ALEX A TRIP TO THE CASUALTY DEPARTMENT . . .

WEB SITE: WWW.FIRESTORM2.CO.UK

FLUFFY

FLUFFY BY NAME,
NOT FLUFFY BY NATURE...

WEIGHT	HEIGHT
97KG	0.2M

LENGTH	SPEED
1.03M	8MPH

WIDTH	CLEARANCE
0.66M	1MM

POWER	WEAPONS
2 x 24V ELECTRIC MOTORS	DOUBLE-ENDED SPINNING AXE

TEAM (LONDON)

PETER HOLROYD (CAPTAIN), PETER JOHNSON AND RICHARD JOHNSON

TEAM BATTLE HISTORY

FIFTH WARS: First-time contender Fluffy caused massive damage to 101 and performed well against Terrorhurtz. They nearly caused a major upset in the heat final by ripping off Pussycat's deadly blade, but suffered very bad luck and broke down.

EXTREME: Competed in UK Mayhem.

BEST MOMENT: Winning the Most Promising Newcomer Award for the Fifth Wars.

WORST MOMENT: Fluffy's breakdown after tearing off Pussycat's awesome blade. They were close enough to the semi-finals to smell them when Fluffy conked out.

WEB SITE: WWW.FLUFFYROBOT.CO.UK

AWARDS
- Most Promising Newcomer Award (Fifth Wars)

Most Violent Battle

When:
Semi-final 2, the Fourth Wars

Contenders:
Hypno-Disc and Splinter

What happened:
Splinter, the underdogs, decided that the best way to attack the hugely powerful Hypno-Disc was to charge straight at them before they had the chance to get their disc up to speed. It worked, so they did it again. But Hypno-Disc decided that enough was enough and it was time to get disc-tructive... They mercilessly ripped off Splinter's front armour, then a side panel, leaving them exposed to further attack. And attack Hypno-Disc did. Splinter were buckled, tattered and torn – and immobilized.

What they said:
Splinter: 'We were going to build another one anyway. Hypno-Disc have done us a favour by taking this one to bits!'
Hypno-Disc: 'Our robot is much stronger and better engineered this time – and we decided not to hold back. Awesome disc-truction.'

Quickest Battle

When:
Round 2, heat G, the Fifth Wars

Contenders:
Evolution and Spawn Again

What happened:
Evolution's robot was modelled on a tank. It had a nice meaty blade, its turret spun 360° and it was made of MDF. It didn't stand a chance. Spawn Again used their legendary flipper to flip Evolution once – up and over they went. Spawn Again flipped for a second time – and Evolution joined the robot wreckage outside the arena wall. It was that simple. From the moment of activation to Evolution's exit from the arena, this battle took just 19.1 seconds.

What they said:
Spawn Again: 'It went exactly to plan. We said we were going to come in here and get them straight out and we did the job straight away.'
Evolution: 'It's time for us to evolve . . .'

GEMINI

FORMER INCARNATIONS: MACE, MACE II

DOUBLE TROUBLE!

WEIGHT	**HEIGHT**
100KG	0.47M
LENGTH	**SPEED**
1.6M	5MPH
WIDTH	**CLEARANCE**
0.68M	15MM
POWER	**WEAPONS**
4 X WHEELCHAIR MOTORS	HIGH-POWERED FLIPPER

TEAM (ST LEONARDS ON SEA)

SHANE HOWARD (CAPTAIN), BRIAN FOUNTAIN AND
DARYL HOWARD

TEAM BATTLE HISTORY

SECOND WARS: (AS MACE) REACHED SEMI-FINALS, HELPING MATILDA TO SPIKE CHAOS EN ROUTE.

THIRD WARS: (AS MACE II) MET UP WITH CHAOS 2 AGAIN IN ROUND 2 OF THE SEMI-FINALS IN A THRILLING BATTLE, BUT THIS TIME WERE FLIPPED AND IMMOBILIZED BY THE SERIES GRAND CHAMPIONS.

FOURTH WARS: KNOCKED OUT BY TORNADO IN HEAT FINAL.

FIFTH WARS: SPLIT UP, THEN TEAMED UP TO PUT RUF RUF DOUGAL IN THE DOG HOUSE. WENT THE DISTANCE AGAINST REACTOR II IN A BRILLIANT ROUND-2 BATTLE, BUT THEIR SELF-RIGHTING MECHANISM FAILED.

EXTREME: COMPETED IN UK ALL STARS.

BACKSTAGE GOSSIP: AFTER THE FIRST PART OF GEMINI WAS BUILT CAME TEST DAY... AT FIRST, THIS WENT WELL, BUT WHEN THE TEAM TRIED THEIR TURBO IT JAMMED ON, AND SENT THE ROBOT FLYING OFF OVER THE NEIGHBOUR'S GARDEN, ENDING UP WHEEL-SPINNING IN A FLOWERBED!

BEST MOMENT: GETTING INTO ROBOT WARS IN THE FIRST PLACE, HAVING SO MANY GOOD FIGHTS AND MEETING ALL THE PEOPLE FROM THE OTHER TEAMS.

WORST MOMENT: WHEN THE SENTINEL IN THE SECOND WARS STOPPED THEM FROM BEATING PANIC ATTACK. ACCORDING TO GEMINI, IF IT HADN'T INTERFERED, THE OUTCOME OF THE WAR MIGHT HAVE BEEN VERY DIFFERENT...

WEB SITE: MEMBERS.LYCOS.CO.UK/TEAM_MACE

AWARDS
BEST-DESIGNED ROBOT (FOURTH WARS) – JOINT WINNERS WITH RAZER
MOST ORIGINAL ENTRY (FOURTH WARS)

HYPNO-DISC

SPIN TO WIN!

WEIGHT	HEIGHT
100KG	0.26M

LENGTH	SPEED
0.98M	10MPH

WIDTH	CLEARANCE
0.56M	2MM

POWER	WEAPONS
ELECTRIC MOTORS	HORIZONTAL SPINNING-DISC

TEAM (MIDDLETON-CHENEY)

DAVE ROSE (CAPTAIN), DEREK ROSE AND KEN ROSE

TEAM BATTLE HISTORY

THIRD WARS: LOST TO CHAOS 2 IN A CLIFFHANGER OF A GRAND FINAL, WHEN THE EVENTUAL GRAND CHAMPIONS FLIPPED THEM.

FOURTH WARS: RAMPAGED THROUGH HEATS, SPLINTERING SPLINTER, THEN SAVAGING WILD THING, BEFORE BEING LICKED BY PUSSYCAT (AND SHUNT) IN ROUND 1 OF THE GRAND FINAL.

FIFTH WARS: TEASED BLACK WIDOW, BEFORE WRECKING THEM IN THE FIRST ROUND, AND THEN TRASHED ATOMIC II. RIPPED OUT BULLDOG BREED III'S SAFETY SWITCH TO WIN THE HEAT FINAL. IN THE SEMI-FINALS, FIRESTORM 3 CONKED OUT AFTER HYPNO-DISC'S FIRST HIT, BEFORE THEY TOOK ON DOMINATOR 2 IN A VERY TACTICAL (AND BORING) FIGHT. IT LOOKED AS IF THEY WOULD BEAT BIGGER BROTHER IN THE FIRST ROUND OF THE GRAND FINAL AND HYPNO-DISC DID COMPLETELY TRASH THEM – BUT WERE THEN PUSHED INTO THE PIT BY BIGGER BROTHER!

EXTREME: COMPETED IN UK v GERMANY, UK ALL STARS AND REACHED ROUND 3 OF THE ANNIHILATORS IN UK MAYHEM.

BEST MOMENT: THEIR ROUND-2 BATTLE AGAINST ATOMIC II IN THE FIFTH WARS! HYPNO-DISC NEARLY LOST IT WHEN ATOMIC II FLIPPED THEM, BUT RECOVERED, SHEARED OFF ATOMIC II'S FLIPPER AND RAN RINGS ROUND THEM.

WORST MOMENT: DISAPPOINTED NOT TO TAKE PART IN THE FINAL BATTLE OF THE FIFTH WARS, BUT HOPED TO MAKE UP FOR IT IN THE PLAY-OFF FOR THIRD PLACE. IT WAS FAST, FRANTIC AND FRENETIC, BUT THEN FIRESTORM 3 PUSHED HYPNO-DISC INTO THE PIT AND DIVED IN THEMSELVES. THE JUDGES ASKED FOR A REMATCH, BUT HYPNO-DISC COULDN'T BE REPAIRED ... ROLL ON THE SIXTH WARS!

WEB SITE: WWW.HYPNO-DISC.CO.UK

AWARDS
MOST ORIGINAL ENTRY (THIRD WARS)

KING B POWERWORKS

Former incarnations: King Buxton, King B3

HIT 'EM HARD

WEIGHT	HEIGHT
96kg	0.25m

LENGTH	SPEED
1.05m	16mph

WIDTH	CLEARANCE
0.74m	5mm

POWER	WEAPONS
36v electric motor	Saw, disc and flipper

TEAM (Havant, Hampshire)

Simon Harrison (captain) and Grant Hornsby

50

TEAM BATTLE HISTORY

SECOND WARS: (AS KING BUXTON – NAMED AFTER A CHARACTER FROM THE MAGIC ROUNDABOUT FILM) BEAT ROBO-DOC IN HEAT, THEN POWERED THROUGH TO SEMI-FINALS. LOST TO ROAD BLOCK IN THE THIRD TASK.

THIRD WARS: (AS KING BUXTON) MET UP WITH RIVALS 101 AGAIN IN HEAT FINAL, THIS TIME GOING UP IN SMOKE.

FOURTH WARS: (AS KING B3) ROUND 2 OF HEAT AGAINST ATOMIC TURNED INTO A SHUNTING MATCH, UNTIL KING B3 CAUGHT FIRE. TAG TEAM WINNERS WITH 101.

FIFTH WARS: IN ROUND 1, NIFTY DRIVING AND STYLISH CONTROL MEANT THAT KING B POWERWORKS WON THE JUDGES' DECISION. KING B WERE OUT IN ROUND 2, WHEN DOMINATOR II'S VICIOUS AXE PUNCHED THEM FULL OF HOLES.

EXTREME: (AS KING B3) COMPETED IN UK TAG TEAM AND VENGEANCE.

BEST MOMENT: WINNING THE TAG TEAM TERROR TITLE IN THE FOURTH WARS WITH KING B3.

WORST MOMENT: LOSING THE TAG TEAM TERROR TITLE IN ROBOT WARS EXTREME. THINGS WENT BADLY WRONG IN ROUND 1, WHEN THE ROBOT SPUN WILDLY OUT OF CONTROL. LATER THIS WAS TRACED TO A MICROSCOPIC CRACK IN THE CIRCUIT BOARD BUT, BY THEN, MORE OF THE ARENA HAD BEEN DESTROYED THAN 101. KING B WERE OUT – IN STYLE!

WEB SITE: WWW.KINGBUXTON.COM

KRONIC 2

FORMER INCARNATIONS: WEDGEHOG,
KRONIC THE WEDGEHOG

A PRICKLY CONTENDER

WEIGHT	HEIGHT
92KG	0.5M

LENGTH	SPEED
1.2M	12MPH

WIDTH	CLEARANCE
0.78M	10MM

POWER	WEAPONS
2 x 12V SINCLAIR C5 MOTORS	WEDGE-SHAPED FLIPPERS AND TITANIUM SPIKES

TEAM (BEER, DEVON)

DAVE LANG (CAPTAIN), JOHN LANG AND
MIKE GARDNER

Team Battle History

First Wars: (As Wedgehog) beaten in heat final by Robot the Bruce.

Fourth Wars: (As Kronic the Wedgehog) lost to Thermidor II in heat final.

Fifth Wars: It started well for Kronic 2, when they flipped King B Powerworks, but their own spikes went up in flames, the electrics failed and they were out.

Backstage Gossip: When testing Kronic 2's new top flipper, the team decided to use a piece of wood — as they had with Kronic the Wedgehog. They aimed, fired... and the wooden block sailed through the air for about twenty metres, narrowly missing a car! They now use heavier missiles...

Best moment: Winning the first round battle in the Fourth Wars with Kronic the Wedgehog. The team expected to be knocked out!

Worst moment: In the Fifth Wars, Kronic hoped to do even better than in the previous series, but were eliminated in the very first round...

Web site: www.kronic.co.uk

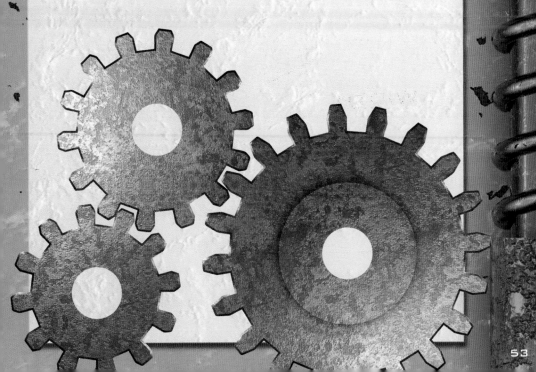

MAJOR TOM
THE GOOD-LOOKING DODGEM CAR!

WEIGHT 90KG	**HEIGHT** 0.89M
LENGTH 1.03M	**SPEED** 10MPH
WIDTH 0.94M	**CLEARANCE** 2MM
POWER 12V ELECTRIC MOTORS	**WEAPONS** VERTICALLY MOUNTED SPINNING FLYWHEEL

TEAM (SHEERNESS, KENT)

HENRY RYAN (CAPTAIN), JOHN MORRIS AND ARTHUR ROBINSON

54

Team Battle History

Fourth Wars: Defeated in round 2 of heat by 101.

Fifth Wars: Played dodgems with Kliptonite in round 1 and made a side-splitting exit from their round-2 match against Kat III (see Funniest Battle on page 90).

Backstage Gossip: Major Tom's latest incarnation was fashioned from a fairground bumper car, retrieved from a field — and his head was originally a bubblegum dispenser!

Best moment: When Major Tom's sponsors gave them three brand-new motors!

Worst moment: When Major Tom was decapitated by Shunt...

Web site: www.majortom.zzn.com

MING III

FORMER INCARNATIONS: MING, MING II

MEAN AND MERCILESS

WEIGHT	HEIGHT
100KG	0.8M

LENGTH	SPEED
1.33M	15MPH

WIDTH	CLEARANCE
1.77M	1MM

POWER	WEAPONS
2 x 12V ELECTRIC MOTORS AND MOTOR-DRIVEN NOSE CONE	HYDRAULIC CRUSHER ARM AND LIFTING ARM AT REAR

TEAM (KETTERING)

ANDREW COTTERELL (CAPTAIN), ALEXANDER COTTERELL AND OLIVER COTTERELL

Team Battle History

Third Wars: (As Ming) hammered by Mortis in round 1 of heat.

Fourth Wars: (As Ming II) made it to round 2 of heat, but were spiked, lifted and then immobilized by The Morgue.

Fifth Wars: Ming III took a pounding, but fought back. Just as it looked as if they might beat Terrorhurtz, Matilda shunted them from behind, even though they were nowhere near the CPZ! Matilda was shown the red card by Ref Bot, but Ming III were damaged and lost on judges' decision.

Extreme: Competed in UK Mayhem and won Vengeance battle against Mega Morg.

Best moment: In the team's opinion, this will be when they reduce Mortis to a pile of spare parts in their next battle, to pay them back for the battering Ming received in the Third Wars. Ever since then, they've been looking forward to revenge.

Worst moment: Fight with Terrorhurtz in round 1 of the Fifth Wars. It was a fierce battle and Ming sustained a lot of damage. Eventually, Terrorhurtz's air supply for their axe ran out, while Ming's crusher weapon was still 100 per cent available. They managed to grab Terrorhurtz in one corner and were slowly winning the tug-of-war towards the flames, when Matilda charged in from nowhere with her newly fitted vertical spinning disc. It ripped out one of Ming's drive motors, completely immobilizing them. Matilda did receive a reprimand, but this didn't make up for losing the fight.

Web site: www.ming.ro

MINI MORG

FORMER INCARNATIONS: THE MORGUE, MEGA MORG

THE ROBOT WITH A DEATH WISH . . .

WEIGHT	HEIGHT
100KG	0.7M

LENGTH	SPEED
1.13M	10MPH

WIDTH	CLEARANCE
0.72M	3MM

POWER	WEAPONS
2 x 12V ELECTRIC MOTORS	SPIKES AND AXES

TEAM (SWANSEA)

DORIAN CAUDY (CAPTAIN), MARK HOOPER AND
DYLAN JENKINS

TEAM BATTLE HISTORY

FOURTH WARS: (As The Morgue) rammed, rolled and eventually immobilized by Firestorm 2 in heat final. Even though Firestorm entered the pit, the judges ruled that The Morgue had already ceased functioning.

FIFTH WARS: (As Mini Morg) failed to make an impact against Kat III and ended up in the pit.

EXTREME: (As Mega Morg) fought with Diótóir in UK Tag Team, but were unable to continue to semi-finals. Diótóir went on to win with substitute Pussycat.

BACKSTAGE GOSSIP: Ming III is the team's number one arch-enemy and they are ready and waiting for revenge . . . !

BEST MOMENT: Becoming joint World Champions with Pussycat and Diótóir in the Tag Team tournament.

WORST MOMENT: Despite being seeded 19, Mini Morg lost to Katerkiller in round 1 of the Fifth Wars. This was due to a severe lack of testing . . .

MORTIS

THE MOST FEARED AND TECHNICALLY ADVANCED ROBOT OF THE FIRST THREE WARS

WEIGHT 100KG	**HEIGHT** 0.36M
LENGTH 0.91M	**SPEED** 12MPH
WIDTH 0.76M	**CLEARANCE** 50MM
POWER ELECTRIC MOTORS	**WEAPONS** AXE AND LIFTER

TEAM (NOTTINGHAMSHIRE AND CAMBRIDGESHIRE)

ROB KNIGHT (CAPTAIN), ARTHUR CHILCOTT AND PAUL FORD

Team Battle History

First Wars: Lost heat final to Recyclopse on a judges' decision. Won Best-engineered Robot Award!

Second Wars: Beat Oblivion to win heat final. Knocked out by Panic Attack in semi-final.

Third Wars: Beaten by Gravedigger in round 2 of heat.

Fourth Wars: Beaten in heat final by Steg 2.

Backstage Gossip: Mortis were involved in one of the most controversial matches in the First Wars, taking part in a heat final against Recyclopse. Although it was an even fight throughout, Mortis definitely had the edge. The end came when they immobilized Recyclopse and then themselves. The judges kept insisting that it was a draw, but eventually went with Recyclopse in what Mortis consider to be one of the most unfair decisions ever!

Web site: www.industrialtechnology.co.uk/1999/oct/mortis.html

Awards
Best-engineered Robot (First Wars)

61

MOUSETRAP

FORMER INCARNATIONS: TRI-TERRA-BOT

A TRAP DESIGNED TO CATCH MORE THAN A MOUSE...

WEIGHT	HEIGHT
95KG	0.45M
LENGTH	SPEED
1.5M	9.5MPH
WIDTH	CLEARANCE
0.7M	10MM

POWER	WEAPONS
24V ELECTRIC MOTOR	SCALED-UP VERSION OF AN ORIGINAL TRAP MECHANISM

TEAM (WITNEY, OXFORDSHIRE)

STAN LAUNCHBURY (CAPTAIN) AND
JASON LAUNCHBURY

TEAM BATTLE HISTORY

THIRD WARS: (AS TRI-TERRA-BOT) TIPPED OVER BY EVIL WEEVIL IN ROUND 1 OF HEAT.

FOURTH WARS: OUTWITTED SUMPTHING AND SWATTED LITTLE FLY TO REACH SEMI-FINALS, BUT WERE UNABLE TO DEFEND THEMSELVES AGAINST STINGER'S DEADLY AXE.

FIFTH WARS: IN ROUND 1, THEY LUMBERED AROUND THE ARENA, FLIPPING THE TRAP, BUT FAILING TO SCORE A DIRECT HIT. WON WHEN SHREDDER BACKED INTO THE PIT. ROUND 2 WAS A MEGA-AGGRESSIVE BATTLE. MOUSETRAP STOPPED S3'S DANGEROUS BLADE, BUT LOST ON A JUDGES' DECISION BECAUSE THEY SUSTAINED THE MOST DAMAGE.

EXTREME: COMPETED IN UK MAYHEM.

BACKSTAGE GOSSIP: IT'S A LITTLE-KNOWN FACT THAT THE BLUE SPRING ATTACHED TO MOUSETRAP DOESN'T ACTUALLY POWER THE WEAPON. IT'S JUST AN OLD PIECE OF HOSE DESIGNED TO LOOK THE PART!

BEST MOMENT: BATTLE AGAINST S3 IN THE FIFTH WARS WAS SUPERB. OK, SO THEY LOST. OK, SO THEY SUSTAINED LOADS OF DAMAGE. BUT THEY PROVED THAT MOUSETRAP COULD TAKE A BEATING AND STILL DISH IT OUT! (AND THE TEAM WERE PRETTY CHUFFED AT BEING FEATURED AND QUOTED IN THE SUNDAY TIMES TOO!)

WORST MOMENT: BREAKING DOWN IN THEIR ROBOT WARS EXTREME BATTLE AND BEING FLIPPED REPEATEDLY BY ATOMIC II BEFORE BEING TAKEN APART BY SIR KILLALOT.

WEB SITE: WWW.JASONLAUNCHBURY.COM/TEAMMOUSETRAP

NAPALM 2

FORMER INCARNATIONS: DETONATOR, NAPALM, SHADOW OF NAPALM

A TITANIUM-HULLED HEAVYWEIGHT

WEIGHT	HEIGHT
100KG	1.08M

LENGTH	SPEED
1.18M	8MPH

WIDTH	CLEARANCE
1.06M	1MM

POWER	WEAPONS
24V ELECTRIC MOTOR	STEEL SPIKES ATTACHED TO ROTARY ARM

TEAM (LONGFIELD, KENT)

DAVID CROSBY (CAPTAIN), VIKKI ALLGOOD AND MICHELLE DAVEY

TEAM BATTLE HISTORY

FIRST WARS: (AS DETONATOR) KNOCKED OUT IN SECOND TASK OF HEAT WHEN THEIR BATTERIES FAILED.

SECOND WARS: NAPALM IMMOBILIZED SIR KILLALOT IN THE HEATS, BEFORE CRASHING OUT OF THE SEMI-FINALS. THEN SIR KILLALOT GOT HIS OWN BACK BY TOASTING THEM OVER THE FLAME PIT IN THE PINBALL TOURNAMENT.

THIRD WARS: BLASTED THEIR WAY TO THE HEAT FINAL, BUT WERE RAMMED TO PIECES BY STEG-O-SAW-US.

FOURTH WARS: (AS SHADOW OF NAPALM) THRASHED BY DOMINATOR II IN ROUND 2 OF HEAT — AND THEN SHUNTED INTO THE PIT.

FIFTH WARS: NAPALM 2 — THE NEW AND IMPROVED ROBOT — MADE LITTLE IMPACT IN ROUND 1 AND NEVER REALLY GOT GOING IN ROUND 2. WILD THING GAVE THEM A GOOD SHUNTING AND SHOVING, UNTIL NAPALM 2 WAS IN THE PIT AND OUT OF THE CHAMPIONSHIP.

EXTREME: COMPETED IN UK MAYHEM, REACHING THE ANNIHILATORS.

BEST MOMENT: THE TEAM CAPTAIN WAS SO CAUGHT UP IN THE ACTION DURING A FIGHT WITH SPIDER AND GEMINI THAT HE DIDN'T REALIZE THAT NAPALM 2 HAD WON. 'WHEN CRAIG ASKED US HOW WE FELT ABOUT WINNING, I JUST LOOKED AT HIM IN ASTONISHMENT!'

WORST MOMENT: THEY WERE TESTING DETONATOR THE DAY BEFORE FILMING WHEN SOMETHING WENT DRASTICALLY WRONG WITH THE ROBOT. IT SUDDENLY SHOT AWAY, CRASHED INTO A FENCE AND BLEW UP... HOWEVER, BY WORKING THROUGH THE NIGHT AND UP UNTIL THE FILMING DEADLINE, THEY MANAGED TO REPAIR THE ROBOT.

WEB SITE: EASYWEB.EASYNET.CO.UK/DCROSBY/

Dirtiest Battle

When:
Round 1, heat H, the Fourth Wars

Contenders:
Wheely Big Cheese,
Prizephita Mach 2 and
Wheelosaurus

What happened:
THIS WAS REAL MELEE MAYHEM! WHILE PRIZEPHITA AND WHEELOSAURUS WENT FOR IT IN A BIG WAY, WHEELY BIG CHEESE DECIDED TO HAVE A GO AT SIR KILLALOT INSTEAD! WHEN THEY SAW THAT THE HOUSE ROBOT WAS NO PUSHOVER, WHEELY BIG CHEESE REVERSED BACK INTO THE REAL FIGHT WITH A CRUNCH, BEFORE SHOVING PRIZEPHITA INTO SIR KILLALOT – AND ATTACKING THE HEAVYWEIGHT HOUSE ROBOT AGAIN! SECONDS LATER, SIR KILLALOT WAS PERCHED ON TOP OF WHEELY BIG CHEESE, WHO COULDN'T FIND THE STRENGTH TO FLIP HIM. AS A FINISHING TOUCH, WHEELY BIG CHEESE DROVE DOWN THE PIT, FOLLOWED BY PRIZEPHITA, FOLLOWED BY WHEELOSAURUS!

What they said:
THE JUDGES DECIDED THAT BECAUSE PRIZEPHITA HAD BEEN IMMOBILIZED FOR 30 SECONDS, THEY WOULD NOT PROCEED TO THE NEXT ROUND.
PRIZEPHITA MACH 2: 'WE'RE DISAPPOINTED, BUT THAT'S HOW IT GOES, ISN'T IT?'

MOST
MEMORABLE
BATTLE

WHEN:
ROUND 2, HEAT H, THE FIFTH WARS

CONTENDERS:
WHEELY BIG CHEESE AND AXE AWE

WHAT HAPPENED:

IT WAS A BATTLE BETWEEN TEAMS FROM THE SAME TOWN – LANGPORT, SOMERSET – SO IT WAS ALWAYS GOING TO BE A STORMER. BUT NO ONE REALIZED THAT IT WOULD BECOME A REAL CLASSIC! AXE AWE MANAGED TO SLAM THEIR OPPONENT JUST ONCE WITH THEIR AXE, BEFORE WHEELY BIG CHEESE FLIPPED THEM SO HIGH THEY COULD SEE STARS AND SO FAR THAT THEY ALMOST LANDED IN ANOTHER COUNTY. IN THIS 12-SECOND FIGHT, AXE AWE SUCCEEDED IN BECOMING PROBABLY THE HIGHEST-FLYING ROBOT IN ROBOT WARS HISTORY!

WHAT THEY SAID:

AXE AWE: 'THEY SAID THEY WERE GOING TO GIVE US EXTRA TRAINING. WE DIDN'T REALIZE THAT FLYING LESSONS WERE INCLUDED!'

WHEELY BIG CHEESE: 'WE'VE BEEN PLANNING FOR A LONG TIME TO FLIP A ROBOT FROM THE MIDDLE OF THE ARENA RIGHT OVER THE SIDE. NOW WE'VE DONE IT!'

PANIC ATTACK
GRAND CHAMPIONS OF THE SECOND WARS

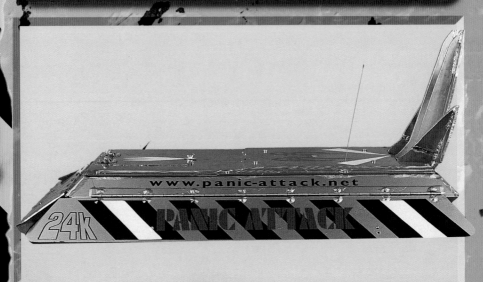

www.panic-attack.net

24k   PANIC ATTACK

WEIGHT	**HEIGHT**
98KG	0.26M
LENGTH	**SPEED**
1M	8MPH
WIDTH	**CLEARANCE**
0.97M	0MM
POWER	**WEAPONS**
24V ELECTRIC MOTOR	LIFTING FORKS

TEAM (CWMBRAN, GWENT)

KIM DAVIES (CAPTAIN) AND MICHAEL DAVIS

TEAM BATTLE HISTORY

SECOND WARS: OVERCAME CASSIUS TO BECOME GRAND CHAMPIONS!

THIRD WARS: MADE IT TO THE SEMI-FINALS, BUT WERE NARROWLY BEATEN BY FIRESTORM ON A JUDGES' DECISION.

FOURTH WARS: SEMI-FINALIST AGAIN, AFTER TOASTING S.M.I.D.S.Y. IN HEAT FINAL. LOST ON POINTS TO STINGER IN ROUND 2 OF SEMI-FINALS.

FIFTH WARS: ONE OF THE MOST EXPERTLY CONTROLLED ROBOTS, PANIC ATTACK STROLLED THROUGH THE HEATS, DISPOSING OF BARBER-OUS, TIBERIUS AND KAT III. REACHED SEMI-FINALS AGAIN, BUT COULDN'T DO MUCH AGAINST PUSSYCAT'S ATTACK IN ROUND 1 AND MADE LITTLE IMPACT IN THE LOSERS' MELEE.

EXTREME: WINNER OF INTERNATIONAL MAYHEM, COMPETED IN UK ALL STARS, REACHED ANNIHILATORS IN UK MAYHEM, WON VENGEANCE BATTLE AGAINST X-TERMINATOR AND WON WILD CARD BATTLE.

BACKSTAGE GOSSIP: PANIC ATTACK MIGHT NOT TAKE THEMSELVES TOO SERIOUSLY, BUT WHENEVER THE ROBOT IS IN THE ARENA, THE AUDIENCE KNOWS THEY'LL SEE A FANTASTIC FIGHT!

BEST MOMENT: BECOMING GRAND CHAMPIONS OF THE SECOND WARS! THE TEAM'S VAN ENGINE SEIZED UP ON THE WAY TO THE FINALS AND THEY HAD TO BE TOWED HOME. THEN THEY RENTED A NEW VAN, EVENTUALLY REACHING THE HOTEL AT 6 A.M. ON THE DAY OF THE FINALS. BY THE TIME PANIC ATTACK FOUGHT, THEY'D HAD NO SLEEP FOR 36 HOURS. AND THEY WON!

WORST MOMENT: DISCOVERING DURING THE THIRD WARS THAT PANIC ATTACK'S BALANCE POINT WAS TOO CENTRAL, WHICH MADE IT TOTALLY UNCONTROLLABLE AND VERY DIFFICULT TO GET IT TO POINT IN THE DIRECTION IN WHICH THEY WANTED TO GO. THIS WAS VERY FRUSTRATING.

WEB SITE: WWW.PANIC-ATTACK.NET

http://rswww.com/panic_attack
PANIC ATTACK PA3

PLUNDERBIRD 5

FORMER INCARNATIONS: PLUNDERBIRD 1, PLUNDERBIRD 2, PLUNDERSTORM, PLUNDERBIRD 4

THERE'S GOING TO BE A PLUNDERSTORM!

WEIGHT	HEIGHT
100kg	0.25m

LENGTH	SPEED
1.2m	13mph

WIDTH	CLEARANCE
0.94m	25mm

POWER	WEAPONS
24v ELECTRIC MOTOR	HYDRAULIC SLICING CLAW AND LIFTER

TEAM (ALTON, HAMPSHIRE)

MIKE ONSLOW (CAPTAIN) AND BRYAN KILBURN

TEAM BATTLE HISTORY

FIRST WARS: (AS PLUNDERBIRD 1) COULDN'T MAKE IT PAST ROUND 1 WHEN THEY GOT CAUGHT ON A GRILLE...

SECOND WARS: (AS PLUNDERBIRD 2) REACHED SEMI-FINALS, BUT WHEN MATILDA KNOCKED OFF THEIR AERIAL, IT WAS ALL OVER.

THIRD WARS: (AS PLUNDERSTORM) DEFEATED IN ROUND 1 OF HEAT BY THERMIDOR (WITH A LITTLE HELP FROM THE HOUSE ROBOTS).

FOURTH WARS: (AS PLUNDERBIRD 4) A MALFUNCTIONING DRIVE DIDN'T HELP IN THEIR ROUND-2 HEAT BATTLE AGAINST KNIGHTMARE, WHO FLIPPED THEM OUT OF THE TOURNAMENT.

FIFTH WARS: PLUNDERBIRD 5 CAME TO AN EARLY HALT WHEN S3 RIPPED OFF THEIR WEAPON AND THEIR ARMOUR IN ROUND 1 OF HEAT.

EXTREME: COMPETED IN UK TAG TEAM WITH BIGGER BROTHER AND WON VENGEANCE BATTLE AGAINST MEGA MORG.

BEST MOMENT: IN THE SECOND WARS, THEY WON THEIR HEAT FINAL AND STORMED THROUGH TO THE SEMI-FINALS. AND ON THE WAY, PLUNDERBIRD 2 BECAME THE FIRST ROBOT TO BEAT TWO HOUSE ROBOTS WITHIN A MINUTE. THIS WAS DEFINITELY THE TEAM'S FINEST HOUR — ALTHOUGH ARRIVING DURING THE FOURTH WARS IN A CHINOOK HELICOPTER (THANKS TO THE GUYS AT RAF ODIHAM) COMES A CLOSE SECOND!

WORST MOMENT: THEY WEREN'T TOO HAPPY AT HAVING TO REMOVE A SAW BLADE FROM PLUNDERBIRD 3 BEFORE FILMING, BUT THE VERY WORST MOMENT WAS THE ROUND 1 MATCH IN THE FIFTH WARS. PLUNDERBIRD 5 GOT SUCH A POUNDING THAT THEY ENDED THE ROUND WITH A CLUSTERBOT. A ROBOT THAT WITHSTANDS SPINNING WEAPONS IS ON THE DRAWING BOARD...

AWARDS
BEST-DESIGNED ROBOT (FIRST WARS)
SPORTSMANSHIP AWARD (SECOND WARS)

PUSSYCAT

FORMER INCARNATIONS: BODYHAMMER

CAPABLE OF DEMOLISHING A GARAGE

WEIGHT	HEIGHT
95KG	0.5M

LENGTH	SPEED
1.56M	14MPH

WIDTH	CLEARANCE
0.74M	100MM

POWER	WEAPONS
24V ELECTRIC MOTOR	PATENTED PUSSYCAT BLADE

TEAM (GLOUCESTER)

ALAN GRIBBLE (CAPTAIN), DAVID GRIBBLE AND
ROBERT BETTINGTON

TEAM BATTLE HISTORY

FIRST WARS: (AS BODYHAMMER) GRAND-FINALISTS, LOSING ON POINTS TO ROAD BLOCK.

SECOND WARS: (AS BODYHAMMER) ELIMINATED DURING ROUND 1 OF HEAT BY SIR KILLALOT.

THIRD WARS: PUSSYCAT WERE DISQUALIFIED BECAUSE THEIR BLADE EXPLODED AND WERE THEN DISCOVERED TO HAVE VIOLATED TECHNICAL REGULATIONS. SCUTTER'S REVENGE WON THE HEAT FINAL, DESPITE GOING UP IN FLAMES . . .

FOURTH WARS: PLOUGHED THROUGH RAZER, THERMIDOR II AND DOMINATOR II TO REACH GRAND FINAL, BUT COULDN'T OUTDO CHAOS 2.

FIFTH WARS: CALMLY DESTROYED EXECUTIONER AND CLAWED HOPPER, BUT IT COULD ALL HAVE GONE BELLY-UP IN THE HEAT FINAL WHEN THEIR BLADE WAS RIPPED OFF BY FLUFFY. HOWEVER, LUCK WAS WITH THE PUSSYCAT TEAM, AS FLUFFY BROKE DOWN. WITH SOME EXPERT DRIVING, THEY RAN RINGS ROUND PANIC ATTACK IN THE SEMI-FINALS, ALTHOUGH IN ROUND 2 THEY WERE BOUNCED AROUND BY FIRESTORM 3 AND LOST ON THE JUDGES' DECISION.

EXTREME: COMPETED IN CHALLENGE BELT, REACHED ALL STARS SEMI-FINALS, WINNER OF UK MAYHEM ANNIHILATOR 1, WON UK TAG TEAM (AS A SUBSTITUTE) WITH DIÓTÓIR AND WON VENGEANCE BATTLE AGAINST RAZER.

BEST MOMENT: KILLING SIR KILLALOT IN ROBOT WARS EXTREME. PUSSYCAT PUNCHED THROUGH THE 280KG HOUSE ROBOT'S BREASTPLATE AND SMASHED THE ENGINE THAT DRIVES HIS HYDRAULICS, CAUSING HIM TO CATCH FIRE.

WORST MOMENT: THE JUDGES' DECISION AGAINST PUSSYCAT AFTER THE FIRESTORM FIGHT IN THE SEMI-FINALS OF THE FIFTH WARS. THE TEAM WAS SPEECHLESS . . .

WEB SITE: WWW.COLDFUSIONTEAM.CJB.NET

AWARDS
SPORTSMANSHIP AWARD (FIFTH WARS)

RAZER

PART BIRD, PART REPTILE, THE REST MACHINE . . .

WEIGHT	**HEIGHT**
96KG	0.39M
LENGTH	**SPEED**
1.06M	11MPH
WIDTH	**CLEARANCE**
0.66M	0MM
POWER	**WEAPONS**
2 x 24 ELECTRIC MOTORS	CRUSHING RAM

TEAM (BOURNEMOUTH)

SIMON SCOTT (CAPTAIN), IAN LEWIS AND VINCENT BLOOD

TEAM BATTLE HISTORY

SECOND WARS: Suffered mechanical failure in third round of heats.

THIRD WARS: Good start against Backstabber, but lost control of self-righting mechanism while fighting Aggrobot in round 2 of heats. Winners of Pinball tournament.

FOURTH WARS: Once again plagued by mechanical problems and knocked out in heat final by Pussycat.

FIFTH WARS: Grand champions! All's fair in love and Robot Wars! In round 2, Razer competed against their partners' robot — Widow's Revenge — where both robots took the plunge into the pit. But Razer was through to the heat final, where they slowly tortured Rick over the flame pit, before foolishly deciding to take on Sir Killalot. Sliced and spiked their way through Spawn Again and S3 in the semi-finals, before beating Firestorm 3 in an exceedingly close fight, taking on Bigger Brother in the grand final — and winning their first UK Grand Championship!

EXTREME: Grand champions of UK All Stars and competed in Vengeance battle, losing to Pussycat.

BACKSTAGE GOSSIP: To fight razer in Extreme Warriors II, Tornado built an anti-Razer frame around their machine with a cutting disc on the front. Razer ripped the weapon to bits, chewed lumps out of Tornado and couldn't believe that the judges' decision went against them.

BEST MOMENT: Winning the Extreme All Stars, the Second World Championships AND the UK Grand Championship for The Fifth Wars — and the huge hug they got from Philippa for the last one!

WORST MOMENT: Breaking down in the Third and Fourth Wars. Imagine how incredibly frustrating it is to have to watch your robot sit motionless in the arena — and not be able to do a thing about it.

WEB SITE: WWW.RAZER.CO.UK

AWARDS
BEST-DESIGNED ROBOT (SECOND WARS)
BEST-DESIGNED ROBOT (THIRD WARS)
BEST-DESIGNED ROBOT (FOURTH WARS)
— JOINT-WINNERS WITH GEMINI
BEST-DESIGNED ROBOT (FIFTH WARS)

ROAD BLOCK

GRAND CHAMPION OF
THE FIRST WARS

WEIGHT	HEIGHT
80.9KG	0.45M

LENGTH	SPEED
1.6M	8MPH

WIDTH	CLEARANCE
1.1M	5MM

POWER	WEAPONS
ELECTRIC MOTOR	REAR-MOUNTED CIRCULAR SAW WITH TUNGSTEN-TIPPED TEETH

TEAM (BODMIN)
HENDER BLEWETT (CAPTAIN), CHRIS KINSEY AND
PETER KINSEY

TEAM BATTLE HISTORY

FIRST WARS: ROAD BLOCK STORMED TO VICTORY IN AN ACTION-PACKED GRAND FINAL AGAINST RECYCLOPSE, CUNNING PLAN, ROBOT THE BRUCE, T.R.A.C.I.E. AND BODYHAMMER TO BECOME THE VERY FIRST ROBOT WARS GRAND CHAMPIONS!

SECOND WARS: WON THE PLAY-OFF IN THE GRAND FINAL TO COME THIRD.

BEST MOMENT: THE A-LEVEL STUDENTS WERE IN NO DOUBT ABOUT THEIR BEST MOMENT – BEATING BODYHAMMER (AND THE NUCLEAR ENGINEERS BEHIND IT) TO BECOME GRAND CHAMPIONS OF THE FIRST WARS. 'ABSOLUTELY MAGNIFICENT.'

WORST MOMENT: FAILING TO WIN THE SECOND WARS. THERE ARE NO PRIZES FOR THIRD PLACE IN ROBOT WARS...

S3

FORMER INCARNATIONS: TRI-TERRA-BOT

A HAMMERHEAD SHARK OF A MACHINE

WEIGHT	HEIGHT
100KG	0.45M

LENGTH	SPEED
0.9M	9.5MPH

WIDTH	CLEARANCE
1.38M	10MM

POWER	WEAPONS
2 x 24V ELECTRIC MOTORS	VERTICALLY MOUNTED DISC AND SNATCH WEAPON

TEAM (SWADLINCOTE, LEICESTERSHIRE)

DAVID BARKER (CAPTAIN), IAN PRITCHARD AND PETE ALLSOPP

TEAM BATTLE HISTORY

FIFTH WARS: RIPPED PLUNDERBIRD 5 TO PIECES IN ROUND 1, THEN BECAME LOCKED IN A DEADLY EMBRACE WITH MOUSETRAP IN ROUND 2, BUT CAUSED MOST DAMAGE AND WON ON A JUDGES' DECISION. IN THE HEAT FINAL, THEY WERE PURPOSEFUL AND MENACING, BUT ONLY WON BECAUSE STINGER STOPPED WORKING. IN ROUND 1 OF THE SEMI-FINALS, S3 WERE PUSHED DOWN THE PIT BY BIGGER BROTHER, BEFORE WINNING A CONTROVERSIAL JUDGES' DECISION IN THE LOSERS' MELEE. IT WAS ONLY A TEMPORARY STAY OF EXECUTION BEFORE RAZER SPIKED THEM, THEN TOASTED THEM OVER THE FLAME PIT IN ROUND 2.

BACKSTAGE GOSSIP: THE TEAM'S FUNNIEST ROBOT WARS MOMENT WAS WHEN THEY DISCOVERED THAT S3 HAD BEEN QUIETLY SMOULDERING AFTER THE BOUT WITH RAZER WHICH HAD PIERCED ONE OF ITS BATTERIES. THE RESULTING SHORT CIRCUIT HAD LITERALLY COOKED THE ROBOT FROM THE INSIDE, WHILE THE TEAM WAS HAVING A WELL-EARNED SNACK. THEY RETURNED TO THE PITS TO FIND THE BATTLE-SCARRED S3 SURROUNDED BY FIRE FIGHTERS! LUCKILY, NO MAJOR DAMAGE WAS SUSTAINED.

WORST MOMENT: TRAVELLING TO NEWCASTLE TO ENTER THE QUALIFYING ROUND FOR THE FIFTH WARS. THEY'D ONLY BOLTED THE WHEELS ON THE ROBOT THE NIGHT BEFORE, SO TESTING AND DRIVING PRACTICE WAS LIMITED TO A VERY SHORT SESSION. S3'S WEAPON WORKED PERFECTLY, BUT THEY DISCOVERED THAT THEY HAD A SERIOUS PROBLEM WITH THE ROBOT'S RADIO CONTROL: THE RADIO RANGE EXTENDED FOR JUST A FEW METRES BEFORE THE FAILSAFES CUT ALL POWER! SOME HASTY ADJUSTMENTS TO THE AERIAL INSTALLATION SEEMED TO DO THE TRICK, BUT THEY HAD NO WAY OF PROVING THAT THE ROBOT WOULD RESPOND CORRECTLY IN A BIG ARENA WITH LOTS OF RADIO INTERFERENCE SOURCES. THE TESTING WOULD HAVE TO BE IN BATTLE . . .

BEST MOMENT: HEADING BACK FROM NEWCASTLE, WITH TWO BATTLES UNDER THEIR BELTS! THEY'D KEPT THE ACTION DOWN THE END OF THE ARENA NEAREST TO THEM, SO THAT THE RADIO CONTROL WOULD WORK!

WEB SITE: WWW.USERS.GLOBALNET.CO.UK/~BARKER03/1LAW.HTM

AWARDS
MOST ORIGINAL ENTRY (FIFTH WARS)

S.M.I.D.S.Y.

SORRY, MATE, I DIDN'T SEE YOU

WEIGHT	HEIGHT
99KG	0.26M

LENGTH	SPEED
1.2M	10MPH

WIDTH	CLEARANCE
0.8M	18MM

POWER	WEAPONS
2 x 24V ELECTRIC MOTORS	AXE AND LIFTER

TEAM (MAIDSTONE, KENT)

MIK REED (CAPTAIN), ROBIN BENNETT AND ANDY PUGH

Team Battle History

Third Wars: Beaten in round 2 of heat by Dreadnought.

Fourth Wars: Rammed Aggrobot II into the side of the arena to reach the heat final, but lost when Panic Attack dumped them into the flame pit.

Fifth Wars: Overpowered Obsidian, then 8645T, before meeting Chaos 2 in a cliffhanger of a heat final. Chaos 2 flipped S.M.I.D.S.Y. against the side of the arena, and then accidentally immobilized themselves. S.M.I.D.S.Y. struggled to get back on the arena floor, but ran out of time and lost on a rematch.

Extreme: Competed in UK Mayhem and UK Tag Team.

Best moment: Sumo in the Fourth Wars. They had to avoid being pushed out of the ring by Shunt for as long as possible. S.M.I.D.S.Y. ducked, dived and dodged away from Shunt's mighty bulldozer blade for a grand total of 14.11 seconds. It wasn't long enough to win the round, but it was long enough to send the crowd wild with their driving tactics!

Worst moment: S.M.I.D.S.Y. have a bad habit of being drawn against previous and current Grand Champions, so their worst moments were when they realized that they'd be competing against Panic Attack in the Fourth Wars and Chaos 2 in the Fifth Wars. But at least they know that they were beaten by the best!

Web site: www.smidsy.net

SIR CHROMALOT

A ROBOT IN SHINING ARMOUR!

WEIGHT	**HEIGHT**
96KG	1.18M
LENGTH	**SPEED**
1.05M	15MPH
WIDTH	**CLEARANCE**
0.64M	5MM
POWER	**WEAPONS**
24V ELECTRIC MOTOR	GAS-POWERED FLIPPER, DRILLS

TEAM (SOUTH OCKENDEN, ESSEX

STEVE MERRILL (CAPTAIN) AND RAY TAIT

TEAM BATTLE HISTORY

THIRD WARS: Reached round 2 of heats after a controversial judges' decision, but weren't so lucky against their next opponent — Bigger Brother.

FOURTH WARS: Steel Avenger forced them on to an arena spike in round 2 of heat F and it was downhill from there — into the pit.

FIFTH WARS: Had an easy round 1 victory over Rohog, but met their match in round 2 with Firestorm, who flipped them almost immediately.

EXTREME: Won Vengeance battle against Plunderbird 5.

BACKSTAGE GOSSIP: Sir Chromalot take part in regular grudge matches with Plunderbird and have toured the country with The Robot Zone — an exhibition of robots from Robot Wars and Techno Games.

BEST MOMENT: Making a grand entrance at Robot Wars! So far, they have arrived in a Rolls Royce, in an artic truck, with four bouncers and their own group of cheerleaders.

WORST MOMENTS: Discovering just days before the Third Wars was about to be filmed that they had a major problem with radio interference. Every time a relay switched in, they started receiving radio signals from the local taxi company...

WEB SITE: WWW.THEROBOTZONE.CO.UK

SPAWN AGAIN

FORMER INCARNATIONS: SCUTTER'S REVENGE, SPAWN OF SCUTTER

REBORN AND READY FOR REVENGE!

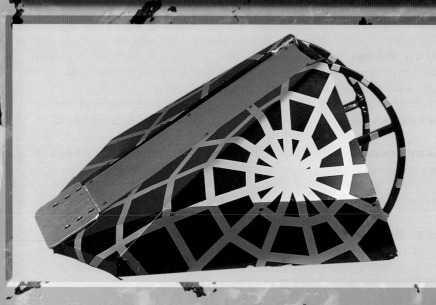

WEIGHT	HEIGHT
84KG	0.82M

LENGTH	SPEED
1.17M	25MPH

WIDTH	CLEARANCE
1.02M	7MM

POWER	WEAPONS
ELECTRIC MOTORS	CO_2-POWERED FLIPPER AND SPIKE

TEAM (EAST TILBURY, ESSEX)

DARREN BALL (CAPTAIN), GRAHAM WARNER AND LUKE JACKMAN

Team Battle History

THIRD WARS: (AS SCUTTER'S REVENGE) BULLDOZED ZEUS
AND THERMIDOR INTO THE PITS, THEN WENT THROUGH TO THE
SEMI-FINALS WHEN PUSSYCAT WERE DISQUALIFIED. WITH THE
HOUSE ROBOTS' HELP, 101 FINISHED THEM OFF.

FOURTH WARS: (AS SPAWN OF SCUTTER) FOUGHT BRAVELY
RIGHT THROUGH TO THE SEMI-FINALS, WHERE PANIC ATTACK
WEDGED THEM AGAINST THE ARENA WALL TO WIN.

FIFTH WARS: SPAWN AGAIN WERE TOO MUCH FOR HYDRA,
THEN BEAT EVOLUTION IN THE QUICKEST ROBOT WARS BATTLE
EVER (SEE PAGE 45). IN THE HEAT FINAL, THEY FLIPPED
DIÓTÓIR, WHO WERE UNABLE TO SELF-RIGHT. SEMI-FINALISTS
ONCE MORE, BUT COULDN'T GET AWAY FROM RAZER, WHO
IMMOBILIZED THEIR FLIPPER AND PUSHED THEM INTO THE PIT.

EXTREME: REACHED SEMI-FINALS OF UK TAG TEAM.

BEST MOMENT: WHEN SPAWN AGAIN FLIPPED EVOLUTION OUT
OF THE RING WITH ONLY THEIR SECOND FLIP OF THE FIGHT.
APPARENTLY THIS WAS PRECISELY THE PLAN!

WORST MOMENT: THEIR EXIT FROM THE THIRD WARS, WHEN
THEY LOST TO 101 AND THE HOUSE ROBOTS...

SPLINTER

FORMER INCARNATIONS: IVANHOE

A CHIP OFF THE OLD BLOCK!

WEIGHT	HEIGHT
96KG	0.65M

LENGTH	SPEED
1.35M	15MPH

WIDTH	CLEARANCE
0.8M	1MM

POWER	WEAPONS
24V ELECTRIC MOTORS	GRABBING ARMS AND PNEUMATIC AXE

TEAM (NORWICH)

STUART WEIGHTMAN (CAPTAIN) AND CRAIG WEIGHTMAN

TEAM BATTLE HISTORY

SECOND WARS: (As Ivanhoe) despite being armed with a lance and axe, they were flipped out of the heat final by GBH.

FOURTH WARS: Powered their way to the semi-finals, but met their match in Hypno-Disc who showed no mercy...

FIFTH WARS: Saw off Viper 01 in round 1, but Bigger Brother flipped them so their self-righting mechanism was dangling over the side of the arena in round 2, and it was time to go home.

EXTREME: Reached round 4 of Annihilators in UK Mayhem.

BEST MOMENT: Before taking part in the Fifth Wars of Robot Wars, the team spent days fiddling with the self-righting mechanism and eventually had to accept the fact that it wasn't going to work. So, when Splinter were well and truly flipped by Bigger Brother in round 2, it seemed as if the Fifth Wars were over for them... until the self-righting mechanism chose that moment to perform and turned them up the right way! After that, they didn't mind losing the fight!

WORST MOMENT: Discovering that they were lined up to fight Hypno-Disc in the semi-finals of the Fourth Wars didn't exactly make Splinter's day. But when, despite a magnificent start, they were splintered into so many bits that the robot had to go home in several carrier bags, they felt a whole lot worse. However, although the body was wrecked, they found that Splinter's insides remained in surprisingly good condition and this fight has been shown so many times on television that it was almost worth the damage!

STEEL AVENGER

WITH EXTRA-TOUGH STEEL POLYCARBONATE ARMOUR

WEIGHT	HEIGHT
100KG	0.8M

LENGTH	SPEED
1.3M	15MPH

WIDTH	CLEARANCE
0.7M	20MM

POWER	WEAPONS
ELECTRIC MOTORS	PNEUMATIC AXE, FRONT BLADE, SPIKES AND REAR FLIPPER

TEAM (COLCHESTER)

JOHN WILLOUGHBY (CAPTAIN), JACKY WILLOUGHBY AND TONY BATES

Team Battle History

Third Wars: Knocked out by Diótóir in round 2 of heat, even though the red fluffy robot was in flames (again).

Fourth Wars: Lost heat final to Wild Thing when their self-righting mechanism failed.

Fifth Wars: Terrified the Tartan Terror in round 1, but fared badly in round 2, when their 20mm clearance allowed Chaos 2 to flip them mercilessly around the arena before launching them out of it.

Extreme: Competed in Challenge Belt, reached round 2 of Annihilators with Suicidal Tendencies and reached final of UK Tag Team, losing to Diótóir and Pussycat.

Backstage Gossip: Building the robot has landed the team's captain in A & E not once, but twice. John Willoughby drew first blood when he ran a hacksaw through his left index finger. A month later, he walked into the edge of a sheet of metal... Clearly, the arena isn't the only dangerous place on Robot Wars!

Best moment: Winning the Best-engineered Robot award in the Fourth Wars. The team knew nothing about it until it was announced on TV. When they heard the news, they leapt around the room as though they had just won the Lottery!

Worst moment: Being hit by Matilda's flywheel at the end of their Mayhem battle with King B and Tornado – when they had already won! 'Cease' had just been called, but Matilda came out of her corner and hit Steel Avenger, sending them through the air and cutting a 3cm gash in the front of the robot. It took them 10 hours' solid work to repair the robot for their place in the Annihilator battle that followed.

Web site: web.ukonline.co.uk/jwrobots

Awards
Best-engineered Robot (Fourth Wars)

FUNNIEST BATTLE

WHEN:
ROUND 2, HEAT J, THE FIFTH WARS

CONTENDERS:
KAT III AND MAJOR TOM

WHAT HAPPENED:
IT ALL STARTED SO WELL FOR MAJOR TOM . . . THEY
STORMED ON THE ATTACK, NEATLY DODGED KAT III'S
DEADLY AXE AND WENT IN WITH THEIR SPINNING
WHEEL. MAJOR TOM JAMMED KAT III AGAINST THE
PIT-RELEASE BUTTON — DAMAGING THE ROBOT AND
OPENING UP THE FLOOR OF THE ARENA IN ONE EASY
MOVE! MAJOR TOM WAS IN CONTROL AND IT WAS
FULL-STEAM AHEAD TO THE HEAT FINAL — AT LEAST,
IT WOULD HAVE BEEN IF THE BUMPER CAR FROM
SHEERNESS HADN'T REVERSED STRAIGHT INTO THE
PIT THEY'D JUST OPENED TO SINK SLOWLY OUT OF
SIGHT . . .

WHAT THEY SAID:
BOTH TEAMS WERE TOTALLY AMAZED BY THE RESULT
AND THE ROBOT WARS AUDIENCE WAS IN HYSTERICS.
AND WHEN THE KAT III AND MAJOR TOM TEAMS WERE
ASKED FOR THEIR THOUGHTS ON THE BATTLE, NO
ONE COULD STOP LAUGHING FOR LONG ENOUGH TO
COMMENT! DEFINITELY THE FUNNIEST BATTLE EVER!

LONGEST-RUNNING GRUDGE

WHEN:
HEAT FINAL, HEAT B, FOURTH WARS
CONTINUED IN VENGEANCE, EXTREME

CONTENDERS:
PUSSYCAT AND RAZER

WHAT HAPPENED:

BATTLE ONE WITH THE SQUEEZABILITY OF RAZER
AND THE BLADE OF PUSSYCAT, IT WAS GOING TO BE A
BATTLE OF TWO ROBOT GIANTS — A BATTLE THAT
RAZER WERE BOUND TO WIN. OR WERE THEY...?
RAZER STARTED WELL, BUT RAN INTO THE ARENA WALL
— AND GOT STUCK! THEY WERE WIDE OPEN TO ATTACK
FROM PUSSYCAT AND THEY WERE WELL AND TRULY
LICKED BY THEIR LIVELY OPPONENT!

BATTLE TWO DESPITE LOSING TO PUSSYCAT IN THEIR
LAST BATTLE, AS WORLD CHAMPIONS, RAZER WERE
STILL THE CLEAR FAVOURITES FOR THE REMATCH. AND
THEY REALLY WENT FOR IT, SPEARING PUSSYCAT,
HOISTING THEM ALOFT AND DEPOSITING THEM ON TO
THE FLAME PIT. BUT PUSSYCAT WEREN'T GOING TO
GIVE UP THAT EASILY. THEY RECOVERED, WALLOPED
INTO RAZER — AND IMMOBILIZED THEM!

WHAT THEY SAID:

PUSSYCAT: 'THEY'RE THE WORLD CHAMPS — IT'S
UNBELIEVABLE THAT WE'VE BEATEN THEM TWICE!'
RAZER: 'WE WANT A REMATCH!'

STINGER

FLY LIKE A BUTTERFLY,
STING LIKE A ROBOT

WEIGHT	HEIGHT
81KG	0.44M

LENGTH	SPEED
1.12M	18MPH

WIDTH	CLEARANCE
0.71M	0MM

POWER	WEAPONS
2 x 24V ELECTRIC MOTORS	BLUDGEONING DEVICE WITH SPIKE

TEAM (LINCOLN)

KEVIN SCOTT (CAPTAIN), KARL SKINNER AND TIM MANN

TEAM BATTLE HISTORY

THIRD WARS: Fought bravely against Mace II in round 1, but lost.

FOURTH WARS: Made it to grand final, but lost on a judges' decision, even though they caused serious damage to Chaos 2's armour and landed some heavy punches.

FIFTH WARS: Sliced and slammed Hippobotamus in round 1, won round 2 when General Carnage ground to a halt, but had a traumatic heat final. S3 immobilized Stinger, a huge flip brought them back to life, but S3 had won.

EXTREME: Competed in Challenge Belt, UK All Stars, UK Mayhem and won Wild Card battle.

BEST MOMENT: Taking part in a last-minute grudge match against Tornado to entertain fans when filming was delayed. Tornado won on a judges' decision, Stinger got trashed, but they had a great time!

WORST MOMENT: Bigger Brother beat Hypno-Disc in the Fifth Wars, but was destroyed in the process. Along with other teams, Stinger offered help with the rebuild. The work was frantic, space in the workshop limited, but everyone piled in to help. In true Carry-On style, as Philippa Forrester came to interview them, Stinger team member Tim's trousers caught fire...

SUICIDAL TENDENCIES

WITH INTERCHANGEABLE WEAPONS . . .

WEIGHT	HEIGHT
100KG	0.7M

LENGTH	SPEED
1.24M	10MPH

WIDTH	CLEARANCE
0.74M	0MM

POWER	WEAPONS
12V ELECTRIC MOTORS	TWIN FRONT SPIKES WITH AXE OR CRUSHER

TEAM (DERBY)

ANDREW JEFFREY (CAPTAIN), ED HOPPITT AND CHARLES BINNS

TEAM BATTLE HISTORY

THIRD WARS: LOST HEAT FINAL TO MACE II WHEN THEY WERE SHUNTED INTO THE HOUSE ROBOTS...

FOURTH WARS: HEAT FINAL WAS AWARDED TO WHEELY BIG CHEESE AFTER A CONTROVERSIAL JUDGES' DECISION.

FIFTH WARS: WON THROUGH TO ROUND 2, AFTER CATCHING RICK IN THEIR DEADLY GRASP, BUT THEN DISCOVERED THAT THEY COULDN'T BE REPAIRED, SO RICK WENT THROUGH ANYWAY...

EXTREME: COMPETED IN UK TAG TEAM WITH STEEL AVENGER, BUT LOST FINAL TO DIÓTÓIR AND PUSSYCAT.

BEST MOMENT: WHEN SUICIDAL TENDENCIES MAKE IT PAST THE HEAT FINAL. THEY ARE DETERMINED TO DO IT!

WORST MOMENT: FAILING TO MAKE IT TO ROUND 2 OF THEIR HEAT IN THE FIFTH WARS, EVEN THOUGH THEY'D BEATEN RICK. THEY JUST COULDN'T FIX THE ROBOT IN TIME – AND WERE DEVASTATED.

THERMIDOR II

FORMER INCARNATIONS: THERMIDOR

A RECIPE FOR MAYHEM

WEIGHT	HEIGHT
97KG	0.34M

LENGTH	SPEED
1.05M	15MPH

WIDTH	CLEARANCE
0.84M	8MM

POWER	WEAPONS
24V ELECTRIC MOTOR	PNEUMATIC FLIPPER AND CLAWS

TEAM (NORWICH)

DAVID HARDING (CAPTAIN) AND IAN HARVEY

TEAM BATTLE HISTORY

THIRD WARS: (AS THERMIDOR) PUSHED INTO THE PIT BY SCUTTER'S REVENGE IN ROUND 2 OF HEAT.

FOURTH WARS: REACHED SEMI-FINALS, FOUGHT BRAVELY AGAINST PUSSYCAT, BUT LOST ON POINTS.

FIFTH WARS: FOUGHT AGGRESSIVELY IN ROUND 1, BUT HAD TROUBLE SELF-RIGHTING AND COULDN'T CLAW THEIR WAY TO VICTORY AGAINST PRIZEPHITA MACH 2.

EXTREME: WINNER OF FLIPPER FRENZY, COMPETED IN UK MAYHEM, THROUGH TO THE ANNIHILATORS, REACHED SEMI-FINALS OF UK TAG TEAM AND WON VENGEANCE BATTLE AGAINST NAPALM.

BEST MOMENT: WINNING THEIR HEAT IN THE FOURTH WARS, BUT THEIR BEST FIGHT WAS AGAINST BEHEMOTH AND STINGER IN ROBOT WARS EXTREME TAG TEAM, WHERE THERMIDOR II FLIPPED BOTH OPPONENTS OUT OF THE RING!

WORST MOMENT: BEING ELIMINATED IN ROUND 1 OF THE FIFTH WARS...

WEB SITE: WWW.TEAMLOBSTER.FREESERVE.CO.UK

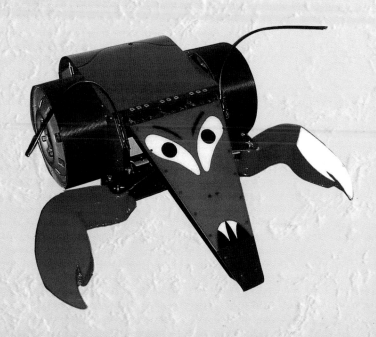

ROBOT PROFILES

TORNADO

CAPABLE OF TOWING A 3-TONNE LAND ROVER

WEIGHT	HEIGHT
100KG	0.25M
LENGTH	SPEED
0.85M	10MPH
WIDTH	CLEARANCE
0.7M	20MM
POWER	WEAPONS
ELECTRIC MOTORS	VERTICALLY MOUNTED SPINNING DISC

TEAM (HUNTINGDON)

ANDREW MARCHANT (CAPTAIN), DAVID GAMBLE AND BRYAN MOSS

Team Battle History

Fourth Wars: Battled through the heats, splitting Gemini in two on the way. The first semi-final was close, with Tornado narrowly beating Wheely Big Cheese, but suffering battle damage. Launched out of the arena by Chaos 2 in the second semi-final.

Fifth Wars: Slammed Gravedigger into the arena wall in round 1, but ran out of steam in round 2 and were pushed into the pit by Diótóir.

Extreme: Winners of Challenge Belt and UK All Stars finalists, beaten by Razer.

Backstage Gossip: Whenever they attend charity events, Tornado is often the first robot sent into the arena to test it – most organizers know that if their arena walls can stand up to Tornado, then they can probably stand up to anything!

Best moment: Winning and holding the Extreme Challenge Belt – Tornado took part in five fights in one day – and didn't break down! Any other Robot Wars team will know what an achievement that is . . .

Worst moment: Bombing out of The Fifth Wars to Diótóir!

Web site: www.teamtornado.co.uk

Awards
Most Promising Newcomer (Fourth Wars)

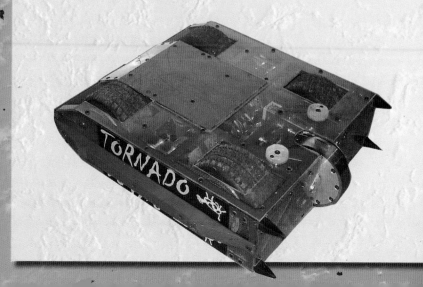

WHEELY BIG CHEESE

FORMER INCARNATIONS: THE MULE, BIG CHEESE

FLIPPING FANTASTIC!

WEIGHT	**HEIGHT**
99KG	0.44M
LENGTH	**SPEED**
1.32M	12MPH
WIDTH	**CLEARANCE**
0.95M	0MM
POWER	**WEAPONS**
24V ELECTRIC MOTOR	ENORMOUS FLIPPER

TEAM (LANGPORT, SOMERSET)

ROGER PLANT (CAPTAIN), JON MCGUGAN AND MURRAY WHARF

Team Battle History

Second Wars: (As The Mule) lost to Plunderbird 2 on points in heat final.

Third Wars: (As Big Cheese) reached heat final once again, but were beaten by Chaos 2.

Fourth Wars: Despite driving into the pit in heat final, won over Suicidal Tendencies as they were declared immobile. In a violent semi-final battle, Wheely Big Cheese lost to Tornado on points, but both robots were very much the worse for wear!

Fifth Wars: Flipped Wolverine out of the arena in round 1, before taking part in a truly fantastic battle when Wheely Big Cheese took seconds to flip Axe Awe. Not even a cheese grater tied to Crushtacean's claw could threaten Wheely Big Cheese in the heat final – after a series of powerful flips, Crushtacean was immobilized and pitted. In their round 1 battle of the semi-finals, they flipped Dominator II sky-high – and then broke down! They didn't deserve to lose.

Extreme: Competed in Flipper Frenzy, UK Mayhem and reached UK All Stars quarter-finals.

Best moment: Their Fifth Wars battle against Axe Awe was one of the most memorable Robot Wars battles ever (see page 67). Wheely Big Cheese flipped their opponents so high that they almost went into orbit!

Worst moment: Not having the funds to take part in series 6...

Web site: www.bigcheeserobot.com

Awards
Best-engineered Robot (Second Wars)

WILD THING

FORMER INCARNATIONS: DEMON, THING

A WHIRLING DERVISH OF A ROBOT!

WEIGHT	HEIGHT
100KG	0.46M

LENGTH	SPEED
0.94M	10MPH

WIDTH	CLEARANCE
0.65M	0MM

POWER	WEAPONS
36V ELECTRIC MOTOR	GIANT CUTTING DISC AND BLADES

TEAM

NICK ADAMS (CAPTAIN), ISABELLE ADAMS AND
JAKE ADAMS

TEAM BATTLE HISTORY

SECOND WARS: (AS DEMON) LOOKED PROMISING, BUT WAS KNOCKED OUT IN THIRD ROUND OF HEAT.

THIRD WARS: (AS THING) FLIPPED BY PANIC ATTACK IN THE SEMI-FINALS, WITH A LITTLE HELP FROM AN ARENA SPIKE...

FOURTH WARS: BEAT STEEL AVENGER IN HEAT FINAL, THEN EXTINGUISHED X-TERMINATOR IN FIRST ROUND OF SEMI-FINALS, BEFORE LOSING TO HYPNO-DISC IN THE SECOND ROUND OF SEMI-FINALS ON A JUDGES' DECISION.

FIFTH WARS: ROUND 1 WAS A BATTLE FOR SURVIVAL AGAINST TROUBLE 'N' STRIFE. HASTY REPAIRS HAD TO BE CARRIED OUT BEFORE ROUND 2, BUT WILD THING DAMAGED NAPALM WITH ITS FIRST THRUST, WINNING EASILY. THE HEAT FINAL WAS VERY CLOSE, WITH THE JUDGES AWARDING THE WIN TO WILD THING BECAUSE OF THEIR AGGRESSION. WILD THING AND CHAOS 2 WENT AT IT LIKE ROBOTS POSSESSED IN ROUND 1 OF THE SEMI-FINALS. CHAOS 2 NEARLY WENT DOWN THE PIT TWICE, BUT ESCAPED AND WON ON A JUDGES' DECISION.

EXTREME: COMPETED IN CHALLENGE BELT AND UK MAYHEM, QUARTER-FINALISTS IN UK ALL STARS.

BEST MOMENT: TAKING PART IN ROUND 1 OF THE SEMI-FINAL WITH CHAOS 2. JONATHAN PEARCE SAID IT WAS ONE OF THE 'MOST BRUISING AND THRILLING BATTLES EVER' — AND THE TEAM WOULD AGREE WITH THAT! IT'S THE BEST FIGHT THEY'VE EVER BEEN IN AND THEY REALLY THOUGHT THAT THEY WERE GETTING THE UPPER HAND TOWARDS THE END.

WORST MOMENT: LOSING THE JUDGES' DECISION IN THE SAME FIGHT.

X-TERMINATOR

THREE, TWO, ONE . . .
X-TERMINATE!

WEIGHT	HEIGHT
100KG	0.58M

LENGTH	SPEED
1.12M	18MPH

WIDTH	CLEARANCE
0.77M	10MM

POWER	WEAPONS
24V ELECTRIC MOTOR	HUGE PNEUMATIC AXE/SPIKE

TEAM (HEREFORD)

MARLON PRITCHARD (CAPTAIN) AND SIMON BALDWIN

TEAM BATTLE HISTORY

THIRD WARS: Reached round 3 of heat, but lost to Panic Attack when CO_2 canisters were damaged, leading to weapon failure.

FOURTH WARS: Got as far as semi-finals but defeated by Wild Thing, who damaged their self-righting arm.

FIFTH WARS: X-Terminator beat Immortalis in an odd slow-motion round 1, but failed to do any damage to Corkscrew in the next round and lost on the judges' decision.

EXTREME: Competed in UK All Stars, Annihilators and Vengeance.

BEST MOMENT: Fighting reigning champions Panic Attack in their Third Wars heat final. X-Terminator were doing incredibly well before it all went pear-shaped!

WORST MOMENT: Getting knocked out in round 2 of the Fifth Wars. The team had done a lot of work to make the axe awesome and had compromised on the robot's mobility by downgrading the batteries to keep it under the weight limit. The batteries packed in and they had to watch most of the fight as sitting ducks.

WEB SITE: WWW.XTERMINATOR.CO.UK

SQUEEZE HANDLE TO VENT CO2

XT

X

THE FIRST WARS: RESULTS

HEAT 1
ROAD BLOCK • KILLERTRON • BARRY • SHOGUN • NEMESIS • GRUNT
FINAL: ROAD BLOCK V KILLERTRON
WINNERS: ROAD BLOCK

HEAT 2
UGLYBOT • SCRAPPER • RECYCLOPSE • DETONATOR • MORTIS • LEIGHBOT
FINAL: RECYCLOPSE V MORTIS
WINNERS: RECYCLOPSE

HEAT 3
CRUELLA • PLUNDERBIRD 1 • WYSIWYG • ROBOT THE BRUCE
WEDGEHOG • DREADNAUT
FINAL: ROBOT THE BRUCE V WEDGEHOG
WINNERS: ROBOT THE BRUCE

HEAT 4
KRAYZEE TOKYO • CUNNING PLAN • BUGS • SAT'ARN
THE DEMOLISHER • VECTOR OF ARMAGEDDON
FINAL: CUNNING PLAN V THE DEMOLISHER
WINNERS: CUNNING PLAN

HEAT 5
WHARTHOG • PSYCHOSPROUT • BODYHAMMER • TORQUE OF THE DEVIL
REALI-T • FULL METAL ANORAK
FINAL: BODYHAMMER V REALI-T
WINNERS: BODYHAMMER

HEAT 6
SKARAB • THE BLOB • T.R.A.C.I.E. • ELVIS • PRINCE OF DARKNESS
EUBANK THE MOUSE
FINAL: SKARAB V T.R.A.C.I.E.
WINNERS: T.R.A.C.I.E.

GRAND FINAL
ROAD BLOCK V RECYCLOPSE V ROBOT THE BRUCE
V CUNNING PLAN V BODYHAMMER V T.R.A.C.I.E.

ALL SIX ROBOTS BATTLE EACH OTHER AT THE SAME TIME.
WINNERS: ROAD BLOCK

THE SECOND WARS: RESULTS

HEAT 1
VICTOR • NAPALM • PANDA MONIUM
PIECE DE RESISTANCE • DEMOLITION DEMON • CALIBAN
FINAL: NAPALM V DEMOLITION DEMON
WINNERS: NAPALM

HEAT 2
MACE • LEIGHVIATHAN • WHEELOSAURUS • DEATH TRAK • TANTRUM • CHAOS
FINAL: MACE V CHAOS
WINNERS: MACE

HEAT 3
CHALLENGER • DREADNAUT • MORTIS • OBLIVION • RAMESES II • GRIFFON

FINAL: OBLIVION V MORTIS

WINNERS: MORTIS

HEAT 4
RAZER • INQUISITOR • MILLY-ANN BUG • BODYHAMMER • BEHEMOTH • ELVIS

FINAL: INQUISITOR V BEHEMOTH

WINNERS: BEHEMOTH

HEAT 5
SPIN DOCTOR • KILLERTRON • PAIN • ORAC • TECHNOPHOBIC • SCHUMEY

FINAL: KILLERTRON V TECHNOPHOBIC

WINNERS: KILLERTRON

HEAT 6
DISRUPTER • PANIC ATTACK • CORPORAL PUNISHMENT • WHIRLING DERVISH
THE PARTHIAN SCOTT • RON

FINAL: PANIC ATTACK V DISRUPTER

WINNERS: PANIC ATTACK

HEAT 7
ROAD BLOCK • KILLER HURTZ • ONSLAUGHT • NEMESIS • R.O.C.S. • LIMPET

FINAL: ROAD BLOCK V ONSLAUGHT

WINNERS: ROAD BLOCK

HEAT 8
STING • LOCO • CASSIUS • GROUNDHOG • RAMPAGE • WIZARD

FINAL: CASSIUS V LOCO

WINNERS: CASSIUS

HEAT 9
KING BUXTON • ROBO DOC • PROMETHEUS • ROTTWEILER • ALL TORQUE
CRUELLA

FINAL: KING BUXTON V ALL TORQUE

WINNERS: KING BUXTON

HEAT 10
TALOS • IVANHOE • KILL DOZER • BROOT • PENETRATOR • G.B.H.

FINAL: IVANHOE V G.B.H.

WINNERS: G.B.H.

HEAT 11
ENZYME • THE MULE • PHOENIX • PLUNDERBIRD 2 • DEMON
MEGA HURTS

FINAL: THE MULE V PLUNDERBIRD 2

WINNERS: PLUNDERBIRD 2

HEAT 12
TENDER CARESS • HAARDVARK • VERCINGETORIX • HAVOC
ANGEL OF DEATH • FLIRTY SKIRTY

FINAL: HAARDVARK V HAVOC

WINNERS: HAARDVARK

SEMI-FINAL 1
NAPALM • PANIC ATTACK • BEHEMOTH • MORTIS • MACE • KILLERTRON

FINALISTS: PANIC ATTACK • KILLERTRON

SEMI-FINAL 2
ROAD BLOCK • CASSIUS • HAARDVARK • KING BUXTON • G.B.H.
PLUNDERBIRD 2

FINALISTS: CASSIUS • ROAD BLOCK

GRAND FINAL

ELIMINATOR 1	ELIMINATOR 2
ROAD BLOCK V CASSIUS	PANIC ATTACK V KILLERTRON

PLAYOFF
ROAD BLOCK V KILLERTRON
WINNERS: ROADBLOCK

FINAL
CASSIUS V PANIC ATTACK
WINNERS: PANIC ATTACK

ROBOT WARS: THE SECOND WARS
GRUDGE MATCHES

JUDGEMENT DAY 1
MORTIS • CASSIUS
WINNERS: MORTIS

RESERVE RUMBLE
LATERAL THOUGHT • MALICE • BUMBLEBOT • JIM STRUTS • FORKLIFT
WINNERS: JIM STRUTS

INFERNO INSURRECTION
SGT BASH • NEMESIS • RAMROMBIT
WINNERS: SGT BASH

SUPER SHOWDOWN
SIREN • KICK ROBUT • BERSERK • DEMON
WINNERS: KICK ROBUT

INTERNET INSURRECTION
GRIFFON • KILLERHURTZ • CORP PUNISHMENT • BODYHAMMER
WINNERS: GRIFFON

JUDGEMENT DAY 2
MORTIS • NAPALM
WINNERS: MORTIS

THE THIRD WARS: RESULTS

HEAT A
BRIMHUR • WEELIWAKO • MACE II • STINGER • RAIZER BLADE • RED DRAGON
FORKLIFT'S REVENGE • SUICIDAL TENDENCIES
WINNERS: MACE

HEAT B
ABADDON • TECHNOPHOBIC • PITBULL • GENERAL CARNAGE • ROBOCOW
BEHEMOTH • SHARK ATTACK • SUMPTHING
WINNERS: PITBULL

HEAT C
AGENT ORANGE • MAX DAMAGE • SPIKE • BLADE • AGGROBOT • BINKY
BACKSTABBER • RAZER
WINNERS: BLADE

HEAT D
SIR CHROMALOT • SHELL SHOCK • BIG BROTHER • GRIM REAPER
MILLY-ANN BUG • BUMBLEBOT • FLIPPER • ULTOR
WINNERS: BIG BROTHER

HEAT E
ANORAKNOPHOBIA • MISS ILE • BIG CHEESE • SHRAPNEL
CROCODILOTRON • CHAOS 2 • HAMMERTRON • SONIC
WINNERS: CHAOS 2

HEAT F
MING • MORTIS • GRAVEDIGGER • MANIC MUTANT • VECTOR • T II
DARK DESTROYER • SGT MEIKLE
WINNERS: GRAVEDIGGER

HEAT G
KATER KILLER • NAPALM • BULLDOG BREED • ROBOPIG • STEG-O-SAW-US
DRAC'S REVENGE • HENRY • HAARDVARK
WINNERS: STEG-O-SAW-US

HEAT H
ALLY GAITOR • CORPORAL PUNISHMENT • BERSERK II • TUTS REVENGE
DEATH WARMED UP • STEALTH • HYPNO-DISC • ROBOGEDDON
WINNERS: HYPNO-DISC

HEAT I
ARMOUR GEDDON • ONSLAUGHT • BEAST OF BODMIN • CRUSHER
VERCINGETORIX • TERRORPIN • INVERTEBRAT • THE WITCH
WINNERS: BEAST OF BODMIN

HEAT J
101 • OVERKILL • CENTURION • EXCALIBUR • ERIC • KING BUXTON
THE IRON MASK • WELD-DOR
WINNERS: 101

HEAT K
AXIOS • PANIC ATTACK • PURPLE PREDATOR • TOE CUTTER • HEFTY
X-TERMINATOR • JUDGE SHRED • MR PUNCH
WINNERS: PANIC ATTACK

HEAT L
UNDERTAKER • PANZER • CHALLENGER II • ATLAS • EVIL WEEVIL
TRITEROBOT • FLIP FLOP FLY • WILD WILLY
WINNERS: EVIL WEEVIL

HEAT M
HAMMERHEAD • PUSSY CAT • CASSIUS II • DUNDEE • SCUTTER'S REVENGE
PLUNDERSTORM • THERMIDOR • ZEUS
WINNERS: SCUTTER'S REVENGE

HEAT N
THING • PRIZEPHITA • CRIPPLER • ALL TORQUE • DAISY CHOPPER • GRIFFON
CERBERUS • KILLERHURTZ
WINNERS: THING

HEAT O
SCHUMEY TOO • STEEL AVENGER • DIOTOIR • STING II • FIRESTORM
CRASH GNASHA • TERMINAL FEROCITY • FACET
WINNERS: FIRESTORM

HEAT P
VICTOR • SCARAB • TRIDENT • TWN TWRN • RATTUS RATTUS • S.M.I.D.S.Y.
DREADNOUGHT • PSYCHOKILLER
WINNERS: TRIDENT

SEMI-FINAL 1
FIRESTORM • PITBULL • PANIC ATTACK • THING • BIG BROTHER • MACE II
CHAOS 2 • TRIDENT
GRAND FINALISTS: CHAOS 2 • FIRESTORM

SEMI-FINAL 2
101 • SCUTTER'S REVENGE • HYPNO-DISC • EVIL WEEVIL
BEAST OF BODMIN • BLADE • STEG-O-SAW-US • GRAVEDIGGER
GRAND FINALISTS: HYPNO-DISC • STEG-O-SAW-US

GRAND FINAL

ELIMINATOR 1	ELIMINATOR 2
CHAOS 2 V FIRESTORM	HYPNO-DISC V STEG-O-SAW-US

FINAL
CHAOS 2 V HYPNO-DISC

WINNERS: CHAOS 2

THE THIRD WARS
SOCCER COMPETITION

GNASHER • MALFUNCTION • VELOCIRIPPA • DEMOLITION DEMON
EVIL WEEVIL • THE ALIEN • THE GENERAL • SPECTRE
WINNERS: EVIL WEEVIL

THE THIRD WARS
WALKER EXHIBITION BATTLES
(NOT A KNOCKOUT COMPETITION)

BATTLE 1
MISS STRUTS V STOMP **WINNERS: MISS STRUTS**

BATTLE 2
MAMMOTH V ANORACHNID **(DRAW)**

PINBALL

DOMINATOR	160	CRUSADER	90
EYE OF NEWT	90	SIX PAC	135
KILLERHURTZ	60	ROCS II	35
OBLIVION II	70	INQUISITOR	70
RAZER	210 (WINNERS)	MORTIS	60

THE FOURTH WARS: RESULTS

HEAT A
CHAOS 2 • ATOMIC • INDEFATIGABLE • MEDUSA 2000 • KING B3 • ATTILA THE DRUM
WINNERS: CHAOS 2

HEAT B
RAZER • ROBOCHICKEN • VELOCIRIPPA • MILLY-ANN BUG • PUSSYCAT • REPTIRRON
WINNERS: PUSSYCAT

HEAT C

FIRESTORM 2 • MORGUE • SCAR • BOLT FROM THE BLUE
DIÓTÓIR • MING II
WINNERS: FIRESTORM 2

HEAT D

STEG 2 • CRUSADER II • CRONOS • IRON AWE • MORTIS • MAZEKARI
WINNERS: STEG 2

HEAT E

101 • DOMINATOR II • HENRY 2 • MAJOR TOM
SHADOW OF NAPALM • DISC-O-INFERNO
WINNERS: DOMINATOR II

HEAT F

WILD THING • HUMPHREY • THE STEEL AVENGER • REACTOR
SIR CHROMALOT • SCORPION
WINNERS: WILD THING

HEAT G

GRAVEDIGGER • THERMIDOR II • KRONIC THE WEDGEHOG • DREADNAUT
WARHOG • DARKE DESTROYER
WINNERS: THERMIDOR II

HEAT H

WHEELY BIG CHEESE • PRIZEPHITA MACH 2 • WHEELOSAURUS • KILLERTRON
SUICIDAL TENDENCIES • MAVERICK
WINNERS: WHEELY BIG CHEESE

HEAT I

KILLERHURTZ • DISTRUCT-A-BUBBLE • SPLINTER • ERIC • CENTURION
SMALL TORQUE
WINNERS: SPLINTER

HEAT J

BIG BROTHER • CLAWED HOPPER • BULLDOG BREED II • HAMMER & TONG
STINGER • SPIKASAURUS
WINNERS: STINGER

HEAT K

EVIL WEEVIL • TIBERIUS • MOUSETRAP • LITTLE FLY • WELD-DOR
SUMPTHING
WINNERS: MOUSETRAP

HEAT L

SPAWN OF SCUTTER • BANSHEE • KNIGHTMARE • VERCINGETORIX
PLUNDERBIRD 4 • FAT BOY TIN
WINNERS: SPAWN OF SCUTTER

HEAT M

GEMINI • TORNADO • KATERKILLER • THE CREATURE • BERSERK 2
INVERTERBRAT
WINNERS: TORNADO

HEAT N

BEHEMOTH • ARNOLD A TERMINEGGER • RAMBOT • JUDGE SHRED II
MILLENNIUM • X-TERMINATOR
WINNERS: X-TERMINATOR

HEAT O
PANIC ATTACK • S.M.I.D.S.Y. • OVERKILL GTI • SAW POINT • AGGROBOT II
OBLIVION
WINNERS: PANIC ATTACK

HEAT P
HYPNO-DISC • PREDATOR • RAIZER BLADE • V-MAX • CERBERUS
TERROR BULL
WINNERS: HYPNO-DISC

SEMI-FINAL 1
CHAOS 2 • STEG 2 • TORNADO • WHEELY BIG CHEESE • STINGER
MOUSETRAP • SPAWN OF SCUTTER • PANIC ATTACK
GRAND FINALISTS: CHAOS 2 • STINGER

SEMI-FINAL 2
PUSSYCAT • THERMIDOR II • FIRESTORM 2 • DOMINATOR II • HYPNO-DISC
SPLINTER • WILD THING • X-TERMINATOR
GRAND FINALISTS: PUSSYCAT • HYPNO-DISC

GRAND FINAL

ELIMINATOR 1	ELIMINATOR 2
CHAOS 2 V STINGER	PUSSYCAT V HYPNO-DISC

FINAL
CHAOS 2 V PUSSYCAT

WINNERS: CHAOS 2

CELEBRITY SPECIAL

ROUND 1

PUSSYCAT (ADAM WOODYAT)	V	IRON AWE (NATALIE CASSIDY)
SIR CHROMALOT (SHANE LYNCH)	V	DISC-O-INFERNO (FIVE)
KILLERTRON (CHRIS EUBANK)	V	GEMINI (ANTHEA & WENDY TURNER)
DIÓTÓIR (VIC REEVES)	V	WILD THING (SHAUNA LOWRY)

ROUND 2

PUSSYCAT V SIR CHROMALOT   GEMINI V DIÓTÓIR

ROUND 3

PUSSYCAT V DIÓTÓIR

WINNERS: PUSSYCAT (ADAM WOODYAT)

PINBALL TOURNAMENT

KILLERHURTZ	235
101	125
HYPNO-DISC	135
GEMINI (WINNERS)	255
SPAWN OF SCUTTER	245
SPIKASAURUS	40
ATTILA THE DRUM	40
BIGGER BROTHER II	180
KING B3	225
S.M.I.D.S.Y.	70
STINGER	75
RAZER	95
BANSHEE	75
DIÓTÓIR	180
FIRESTORM 2	185
INVERTERBRAT	95

SUMO TOURNAMENT

MAVERICK	9
DIÓTÓIR	4
FIRESTORM II	4
S.M.I.D.S.Y.	14
SPAWN OF SCUTTER (WINNERS)	80
X-TERMINATOR	60
SCORPION	7
RAZER	7
BIGGER BROTHER II	4

TAG TEAM

ROUND 1

FIRESTORM II **AND** SCORPION V BIGGER BROTHER II **AND** PLUNDERBIRD 4
INVERTERBRAT **AND** X-TERMINATOR V KING B3 **AND** 101

ROUND 2

FIRESTORM II **AND** SCORPION V KING B3 **AND** 101

WINNERS: KING B3 AND 101

PLAYOFF

BIGGER BROTHER II **AND** PLUNDERBIRD 4 V INVERTERBRAT **AND** X-TERMINATOR

WINNERS: BIGGER BROTHER II AND PLUNDERBIRD 4

ANNIHILATOR – NORTH

SPIKASAURUS • KILLERHURTZ • DOMINATOR II • STINGER
CHAOS 2 • SUICIDAL TENDENCIES
WINNERS: SPIKASAURUS

ANNIHILATOR – SOUTH

VERCINGETORIX • ATTILA THE DRUM • ONSLAUGHT • RAZER
SPAWN OF SCUTTER • BEHEMOTH
WINNERS: RAZER

WAR OF INDEPENDENCE

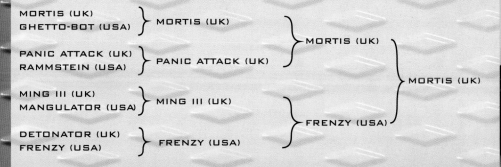

MORTIS (UK)
GHETTO-BOT (USA) ⟩ MORTIS (UK)

PANIC ATTACK (UK)
RAMMSTEIN (USA) ⟩ PANIC ATTACK (UK) ⟩ MORTIS (UK)

MING III (UK)
MANGULATOR (USA) ⟩ MING III (UK) ⟩ MORTIS (UK)

DETONATOR (UK)
FRENZY (USA) ⟩ FRENZY (USA) ⟩ FRENZY (USA)

THE FIFTH WARS: RESULTS

HEAT A

CHAOS 2 • STORM • THE STEEL AVENGER • THE TARTAN TERROR • B645T
T-BONE • S.M.I.D.S.Y. • OBSIDIAN
WINNERS: CHAOS 2

HEAT B

HYPNO-DISC • BLACK WIDOW • ATOMIC II • KAN OPENER • WOWOT • LAMBSY
JUGGERNOT II • BULLDOG BREED II
WINNERS: HYPNO-DISC

HEAT C

STINGER • HIPPOBOTOMUS • GENERAL CARNAGE 2 • GUZUNDERBOT • S3
PLUNDERBIRD 5 • MOUSETRAP • SHREDDER
WINNERS: S3

HEAT D
FIRESTORM 3 • BEE-CAPITATOR • SIR CHROMALOT • ROHOG • BOT OUT OF HELL
REACTOR II • GEMINI • RUF RUF DOUGAL
WINNERS: FIRESTORM 3

HEAT E
WILD THING • TROUBLE 'N' STRIFE • NAPALM • WARHOG • VELOCIRIPPA
THE ALIEN • PRIZEPHITA MACH 2 • THERMIDOR II
WINNERS: WILD THING

HEAT F
DOMINATOR II • DEREK • KING B POWERWORKS • KRONIC 2 • 13 BLACK
CORKSCREW • X-TERMINATOR • IMMORTALIS
WINNERS: DOMINATOR II

HEAT G
TORNADO • GRAVEDIGGER • DIÓTÓIR • DOME • SPAWN AGAIN • EVOLUTION
SABRE TOOTH • HYDRA
WINNERS: SPAWN AGAIN

HEAT H
WHEELY BIG CHEESE • WOLVERINE • AXE AWE • GRANNY'S REVENGE
ROBOCHICKEN-EVO • CRUSHTACEAN • BEHEMOTH • SUPERNOVA
WINNERS: WHEELY BIG CHEESE

HEAT I
SPLINTER • VIPER D1 • BIGGER BROTHER • TIP-TOP • ONSLAUGHT • TETANUS
3 STEGS TO HEAVEN • ELEVEN
WINNERS: BIGGER BROTHER

HEAT J
MINI MORG • KAT III • MAJOR TOM • KLIPTONITE • TIBERIOUS II • MONAD
PANIC ATTACK • BARBER-OUS
WINNERS: PANIC ATTACK

HEAT K
RAZER • BIG NIPPER • SUMPTHING • WIDOW'S REVENGE • AXE-C-DENT
DESTRUCT-A-BUBBLE • RICK • SUICIDAL TENDENCIES
WINNERS: RAZER

HEAT L
PUSSYCAT • THE EXECUTIONER • CLAWED HOPPER • TWISTER • TERRORHURTZ
MING III • FLUFFY • 101
WINNERS: PUSSYCAT

SEMI-FINAL 1
CHAOS 2 • WILD THING • BIGGER BROTHER • S3 • RAZER • SPAWN AGAIN
GRAND FINALISTS: BIGGER BROTHER • RAZER

LOSERS' MELEE
WILD THING • S3 • SPAWN AGAIN

SEMI-FINAL 2
WHEELY BIG CHEESE • DOMINATOR II • HYPNO-DISC • FIRESTORM 3
PANIC ATTACK • PUSSYCAT
GRAND FINALISTS: HYPNO-DISC

LOSERS' MELEE
WHEELY BIG CHEESE • FIRESTORM 3 • PANIC ATTACK
GRAND FINALISTS: FIRESTORM 3

GRAND FINAL

ELIMINATOR 1
BIGGER BROTHER v HYPNO-DISC

ELIMINATOR 2
RAZER v FIRESTORM III

PLAYOFF
FIRESTORM 3 v HYPNO-DISC
WINNERS: FIRESTORM 3

FINAL
BIGGER BROTHER V RAZER
WINNERS: RAZER

EXTREME: RESULTS

ARMED FORCES MELEE
MEGA-HURTS (NAVY) • ANVIL (RAF) • RHINO (ARMY)
WINNERS: ANVIL

UK V NETHERLANDS
PHILLIPER (NETHERLANDS) • CHAOS 2 (UK) • ALIEN DESTRUCTOR (NETHERLANDS)
WINNERS: CHAOS 2

GERMAN MELEE
ANSGAR • NASTY WARRIOR • FLENSBURGER POWER • GOLEM
WINNERS: ANSGAR

FLIPPER FRENZY
CHAOS 2 • THERMIDOR II • WHEELY BIG CHEESE • BIGGER BROTHER
WINNERS: THERMIDOR II

INTERNATIONAL MAYHEM
PANIC ATTACK (UK) • FLENSBURGER POWER (GERMANY)
MAXIMILL (HOLLAND) • MANTA (USA)
WINNERS: PANIC ATTACK

UK V GERMANY
HYPNO-DISC (UK) • NASTY WARRIOR (GERMANY)
WINNERS: NASTY WARRIOR

CHALLENGE BELT
BEHEMOTH • THE STEEL AVENGER • STINGER • TORNADO • COMENGETORIX
WILD THING • CHAOS II • PUSSYCAT
WINNERS: TORNADO

UK ALL STARS

BATTLE 1	CHAOS 2 V X-TERMINATOR	WINNERS: CHAOS 2
BATTLE 2	DIÓTÓIR V WHEELY BIG CHEESE	WINNERS: WHEELY BIG CHEESE
BATTLE 3	PANIC ATTACK V FIRESTORM	WINNERS: FIRESTORM
BATTLE 4	HYPNO-DISC V BEHEMOTH	WINNERS: BEHEMOTH
BATTLE 5	WILD THING V DOMINATOR II	WINNERS: WILD THING
BATTLE 6	TORNADO V 3 STEGS TO HEAVEN	WINNERS: TORNADO
BATTLE 7	RAZER V GEMINI	WINNERS: RAZER
BATTLE 8	PUSSYCAT V STINGER	WINNERS: PUSSYCAT

ALL STARS QUARTER-FINALS

BATTLE 1	WHEELY BIG CHEESE V CHAOS 2	WINNERS: CHAOS 2
BATTLE 2	FIRESTORM V WILD THING	WINNERS: FIRESTORM
BATTLE 3	RAZER V BEHEMOTH	WINNERS: RAZER
BATTLE 4	PUSSYCAT V TORNADO	WINNERS: TORNADO

ALL STARS SEMI-FINALS
BATTLE 1   RAZER V FIRESTORM   WINNERS: RAZER
BATTLE 2   CHAOS 2 V TORNADO   WINNERS: TORNADO

ALL STARS FINALS
RAZER V TORNADO   WINNERS: RAZER

UK MAYHEM

ATOMIC • FIGHTING TORQUE • MOUSETRAP
WINNERS: ATOMIC (FIGHTING TORQUE TO GO THROUGH AS ATOMIC PULLED OUT)

SPLINTER • KILLERTRON • AGGROBOT
WINNERS: SPLINTER

HYPNO-DISC • MING III • WHEELY BIG CHEESE
WINNERS: HYPNO-DISC

BULLDOG BREED • JUDGE SHRED • SPIRIT OF KNIGHTMARE
WINNERS: BULLDOG BREED (SPIRIT OF KNIGHTMARE TO GO THROUGH AS
BULLDOG BREED PULLED OUT)

PUSSYCAT • S.M.I.D.S.Y. • SUMPTHING
WINNERS: PUSSYCAT

VELOCIRIPPA • COMENGETORIX • DISC-O-INFERNO
WINNERS: DISC-O-INFERNO

THERMIDOR II • BEHEMOTH • STINGER
WINNERS: THERMIDOR II

CATACLYSMIC VARIABOT • PANZERWRATH • X-TERMINATOR
WINNERS: X-TERMINATOR

NAPALM • SPIDER • GEMINI
WINNERS: NAPALM

PANIC ATTACK • SHEAR KHAN • DIÓTÓIR
WINNERS: PANIC ATTACK

WILD THING • ARNOLD A TERMINEGGER • FLUFFY
WINNERS: ARNOLD A TERMINEGGER

BEST MAYHEM
STEEL AVENGER • TORNADO • KING B3
WINNERS: STEEL AVENGER

ANNIHILATOR 1
PUSSYCAT • SPLINTER • X-TERMINATOR • HYPNO-DISC • THERMIDOR II
ARNOLD A TERMINEGGER
WINNERS: PUSSYCAT

ANNIHILATOR 2
DISC-O-INFERNO • THE STEEL AVENGER • FIGHTING TORQUE • PANIC ATTACK
NAPALM • SPIRIT OF KNIGHTMARE
WINNERS: SPIRIT OF KNIGHTMARE

UK TAG TEAM

BATTLE 1
KING B3 AND 101 V DIÓTÓIR AND MEGA MORGUE
WINNERS: DIÓTÓIR AND MEGA MORGUE

BATTLE 2
MAJOR TOM AND BIGGER BROTHER V COMENGETORIX AND SPAWN AGAIN
WINNERS: COMENGETORIX AND SPAWN AGAIN

BATTLE 3
CERBERUS AND THERMIDOR II V S.M.I.D.S.Y. AND SUMPTHING
WINNERS: CERBERUS AND THERMIDOR II

BATTLE 4
NAPALM AND SIR CHROMALOT V STEEL AVENGER AND SUICIDAL TENDENCIES
WINNERS: STEEL AVENGER AND SUICIDAL TENDENCIES

SEMI-FINAL 1
STEEL AVENGER AND SUICIDAL TENDENCIES V CERBERUS AND THERMIDOR II
WINNERS: STEEL AVENGER AND SUICIDAL TENDENCIES

SEMI-FINAL 2

DIÓTÓIR AND PUSSYCAT (SUBSTITUTE) V COMENGETORIX AND SPAWN AGAIN
WINNERS: DIÓTÓIR AND PUSSYCAT (SUBSTITUTE)

FINAL
DIÓTÓIR AND PUSSYCAT (SUBSTITUTE) V STEEL AVENGER AND SUICIDAL TENDENCIES
WINNERS: DIÓTÓIR AND PUSSYCAT (SUBSTITUTE)

VENGEANCE

TORNADO V STINGER	WINNERS: TORNADO
X-TERMINATOR V PANIC ATTACK	WINNERS: PANIC ATTACK
RAZER V PUSSYCAT	WINNERS: PUSSYCAT
FIRESTORM V DIÓTÓIR	WINNERS: FIRESTORM
PLUNDERBIRD 5 V SIR CHROMALOT	WINNERS: SIR CHROMALOT
KING B3 V 101	WINNERS: 101
MING III V MEGA MORG	WINNERS: MING III
PLUNDERBIRD 5 V MEGA MORG	WINNERS: PLUNDERBIRD 5
BIGGER BROTHER V COMENGETORIX	WINNERS: BIGGER BROTHER
THERMIDOR II V NAPALM	WINNERS: THERMIDOR II

ANTWEIGHT MELEE
PANTS • LITTLE NIPPER • COMBAT ANT • ANTO • LEGION • ANTY B • RAZZLER
WINNERS: ANTY B

MIDDLEWEIGHT MELEE
GENESIS • TYPHOON • HARD CHEESE • MAMMOUTH • DOOM • ZAP
WINNERS: TYPHOON

FEATHERWEIGHT MELEE
R C WARRIOR • BEEF-CAKE
WINNERS: BEEF-CAKE

WILD CARD WARRIORS
KING B3 • ANTHRAX
WINNERS: KING B3

DOMINATOR II • THE EXECUTIONER
WINNERS: DOMINATOR II

PANIC ATTACK • AXE AWE
WINNERS: PANIC ATTACK

STINGER • AJJAY
WINNERS: STINGER

BEHEMOTH • THE SPIDER
WINNERS: BEHEMOTH

UK HOUSE ROBOT CHALLENGE
STINGER • PLUNDERBIRDS • SCORPION

HOUSE ROBOTS
SHUNT • DEAD METAL • MATILDA

Heat A

RAZER

WELD-DOR 3

RAGING REALITY

BRUTUS MAXIMUS

W.A.S.P.

CYRAX

TETANUS II

RUF RUF DOUGAL

Heat B

FIRESTORM IV

CEDRIC SLAMMER

BARBARIC RESPONSE

X-TERMINATOR

MEGA HURTS 2

SPIRIT OF SCORPION

ROBOCHICKEN

COLOSSUS

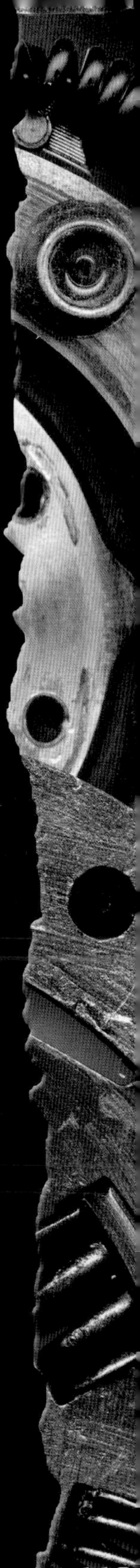

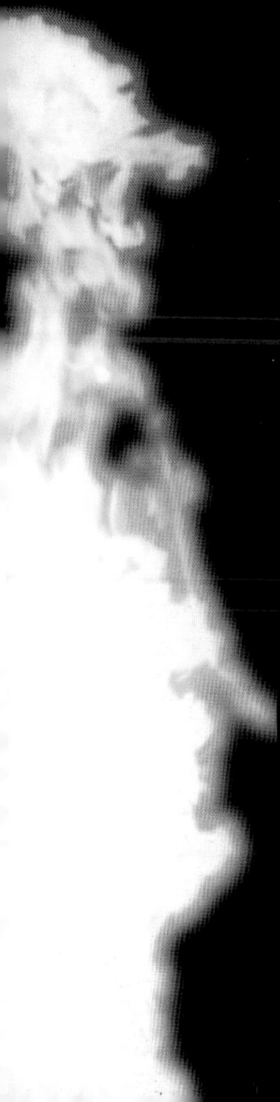

HEAT C

CHAOS 2

DANTOMKIA

DESTRUCTOSAUR

DOCTOR FIST

CRUSHTACEAN

IRON AWE 2

MR NASTY

MIGHTY MOUSE

HEAT D

S3

SIR CHROMALOT

THE ALIEN

ROOBARB

ARMADRILLO

G.B.H. 2

SHREDDER

ICU

Heat E

WILD THING

INFINITY

VADER

INFERNAL CONTRAPTION

259

UFO

THE STAG

AGGROBOT III

Heat F

STINGER

DOUBLE TROUBLE

THERMIDOR II

FLUFFY

DEMOLITION MAN

KAN-OPENER

13 BLACK

CHOMPALOT

Heat G

TORNADO

EDGE HOG

JUDGE SHRED 2½

INSHREDDABLE

REVOLUTION 2

ANARCHY

THOR

TERROR-BULL

Heat H

SPAWN AGAIN

SUPERNOVA

THE HASSOCKS HOG

TIBERIUS III

SHORT CIRCUIT

MING III

SPAM

HOT PANTS

Heat I

PANIC ATTACK

R.O.C.S.

REPTIRRON THE SECOND

CORKSCREW

SABRE TOOTH

KRONIC 2

TERRORHURTZ

A-KILL

Heat J

DOMINATOR II

HYDRA

WARHOG

ST AGRO

S.M.I.D.S.Y.

SUMPTHING

AXE-C-DENT II

COMENGETORIX

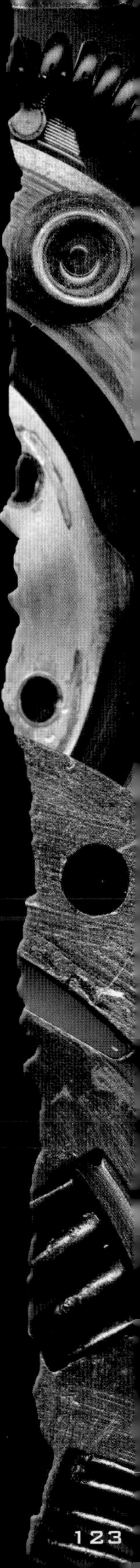

Heat K

HYPNO-DISC

REVENGE OF TROUBLE
AND STRIFE

KAT3

4X4

GRANNY'S REVENGE II

BARBER-OUS II

SPIN DOCTOR

BULLDOG BREED

Heat L

BIGGER BROTHER

BEHEMOTH

MAJOR TOM

TRIDENTATE

DEREK 2

KILLER CARROT 2

DISC-O-INFERNO

RIPTILION